A Hickli
Marshman's Diary

of reed and sedge cutting in the 1980s

by
Gerald Nudd

Contents

Acknowledgements

Gerald Nudd kept a day-to-day diary between 1980 and early 1987 mainly of what he saw and did while reed and sedge cutting in the Hickling, Horsey, Brograve, Brayden, Martham and Blackfleet Broad areas of East Norfolk. In fact there is a lot more in the diaries - including watching over nature, helping friends and colleagues, shooting and going sea fishing off the Norfolk coast.

The diaries came into the possession of his brother Roger Nudd after Gerald's death in 1999. Together with photographs which Roger accumulated from family and friends, and Roger's own sketches of birds, this book of extracts from the diaries has been put together.

Christine Cleveland transcribed the diaries just as they had been written by Gerald - leaving spelling and punctuation as he wrote it. The introduction was written by David Cleveland, along with much assistance from Roger Nudd, Hazel Nudd, Jack Aldred, Paul Borrett, Robin Buxton, Paula Cooper, Michael Nicholls, Mike Page, James Perry, and Richard Starling.

Published by David Cleveland   Manningtree 2019
ISBN 978-1-9993672-1-3

British Library Cataloguing-in-Publication Data
A catalogue record for this book is available from the British Library

Designed by Charlotte Cleveland

Printed in Great Britain by The Lavenham Press Ltd.

Also published by David Cleveland:
A Look Back at The Broads 2019

Cover picture: Stacking reed at Horsey Staithe on 1st June 1984.
Title page: Gerald carrying bundles of reed and smoking at the same time.
This photograph was taken 6th December 1983, an early start for reed cutting.

Gerald Nudd.

Introduction

Gerald Robert Nudd was born in Hickling in 1940. He was mainly a reed and sedge cutter working the wide open marshes of East Norfolk in the 1970s, 1980s and 1990s, a place of dykes and drains and much wildlife. Gerald noticed everything going on around him as he cut reed for thatching in the winter months, and sedge for the roof capping for much of the rest of the year. He kept a diary noting the weather, water levels, plants and insects, and birds and other wildlife around him. Now and then he would comment on the quality of the reed, and incidental things such as other reed cutters - "Billy [Nicholls] and Brian [Applegate] had their reed stolen at mautby level yesterday" [10th May 1984] and that he went sea fishing at Eccles [near Sea Palling] and caught "two mackerel 1 pint shrimps. No skate on the line. About thirty scooters came from the north going south. Four gannets. One red admiral butterfly heading out to sea. Terns hunting whitebait" [8th July 1984]. Longshoring was one of his pastimes, which brought in a bit of extra cash.

With his three brothers Gerald lived at the family home which was No. 7 The Green at Hickling. This was one of eighteen council houses built about 1937 and a few after the war in a circular arrangement with a concrete road locally known as The Track. Their father, Charles Nudd, born in 1908, was a marshman and Broadsman who did a bit of reed cutting and sedge cutting now and then and other jobs around boats, marshes, the rivers and Broads. Charles was one of nine children of Cubit and Thirza Nudd, who were married on 10th June 1891 in Hickling Church. Their children were Cubit

1

Nudd (1891-1945) a marshman; Alfred Nudd (1894-1985) sea fisherman; Joshua Nudd (1896-1980) marshman and seaman; Reginald Nudd (1897-1980) agricultural worker at Horsey; Lovewell Nudd who lived less than a year (1899-1899); Norah Nudd (1903-1979) who married Arthur Adams from Potter Heigham; Jack Nudd (1905-1980) marshman and seaman; the diarist's father Charles (1908-1982) who latterly worked at Richardson's boat yard at Stalham; and Ruby Nudd (1913-1997) who married Alexander Goodwin, a farm worker.

Charles married Evelyn Bell (1915-1997) in 1937, and they had four sons - Michael Nudd born in 1938, our diarist Gerald Nudd born in 1940, Roger Nudd born in 1943 and Austin Nudd born in 1946.

Gerald and his brothers all went to Hickling Primary School, then on to the Secondary Modern School at Stalham. Michael did National Service, then became a painter and decorator. Roger worked as a Broadsman like his father, learning at several yards before spending 35 years at Richardson's at Stalham. Austin became a fitter at the Crane Fruehauf factory in North Walsham.

Carrying bunches of sedge off the marshes.

Gerald Nudd first spent several years as a deckhand working on some of the last of the herring boats out of Lowestoft, then going to Cairo and the Sudan in 1961 assisting on a shellfish project for six months, then coming back to Hickling where he did odd farm jobs at first, then became a self-employed marshman. For some years from 1978 he helped look after an eel set in Kendal Dyke with local men Robin Myhill [boat builder, Broadsman, and sportsman] and Chris Nudd [Broadsman, eel set operator, painter and decorator]. This also brought in a little extra money.

The brothers continued to live at No. 7 The Green until Michael left to get married in 1964 and Roger set up home with his partner Susan Gayfer in 1980. Gerald and Austin remained living at home. Their father died in 1982, and the two brothers looked after their mother until she died in 1997. Gerald and Austin continued to live at home. Gerald died on January 13th 1999. Austin remained at No. 7 for about another year, then moved to 22 Barnfield Close in Hickling where he died in 2011.

Gerald never had a car, he biked and walked everywhere. He called his bicycle his 'Mare of Steel'. Gerald was a very social person, having many friends whom he enjoyed meeting, along with his work colleagues, in the *Greyhound* or the *Pleasure Boat Inn*, both in Hickling. He came from a long line of Nudds living in the Hickling area, so had many relations in and around the village. He never married.

It was reed cutting and sedge work on the marshes that occupied most of his working life, work that he enjoyed as his diaries reveal. Reed cutting took place in the winter months, mostly during January - sometimes it started earlier - February and March, stopping as soon as the colts (new reed shoots) were coming through. These would be next year's crop and had to be left to grow. Then it was mainly cutting and gathering the pliable sedge through to October or thereabouts. Gerald often had to stop when the water level was too high, when birds were nesting or for other reasons, so he filled in with other work, such as boat maintenance, helping friends with projects, a bit of building work, or working for John Buxton of Horsey Hall.

During the late autumn, and at other quiet times, or when he simply took a day off, he would look after an eel set at Kendal Dyke, or go sea fishing off Eccles in a small boat belonging to Tim Cox [boatyard owner at Barton Turf], and together they would go long-lining - setting a line of baited hooks - or netting for herring. Occasionally he went shooting. "….went shooting on Jim Perrys farm. 11 pheasants one hare. One jay." [10th December 1983]. Perry's Poplar Farm was by the Sutton Road in Hickling.

Houses along 'The Track' at Hickling Green. Gerald Nudd lived at No. 7.
This picture taken in August 2019.

Reed cutting and sedge cutting, and generally clearing up the marshes, was hard physical work. After cutting the reed or sedge it had to be transported to a convenient place such as Horsey, Hickling or Somerton staithes to be stored and collected by the buyer. Gerald's working companions reed and sedge cutting were mainly George Newman and Billy Nicholls, along with Brian Applegate, Richard Starling and others - all local men earning a living one way or another from the Broadland marshes, and other jobs here and there.

Between 1980 and 1987 Gerald Nudd wrote short sequences at the end of each day of what he had seen, heard, and done in a set of diaries and note books. Thanks to his brother Roger, a number of these have survived. Gerald's observational writings give us a feeling of being out in the open, in keen fresh air, the sun on our faces, the only sounds being the birds, the wind and rustling reeds. At other times we feel the severe cold as he describes frozen dykes, frost on the reeds lingering all day, and snow showers as well.

He uses local names such as Starch Grass, and area of reed and sedge north west of Martham Broad; 'Kings marshes' - those worked by tenant farmer Ernie King on the Buxton Estate; of 'Gibbs outlet' - the dyke from Eastfield pump taking water across the Brayden marshes to Waxham Cut; of the 'Warbush', an area of marsh north side of Catfield dyke, and many other names that only local people would know about. Brayden marshes next to Horsey Mere he calls 'Breydon' in the diaries (not to be confused with Breydon Water at the back of Yarmouth) - an example of his personal spelling.

Incidentally there was once a tower windmill pumping water from Hickling marshes near Eastfield Farm, sending the water down the outlet and across Brayden marshes to fall into Waxham Cut. Since the 1840s this Eastfield Drainage Mill was looked after by the Gibbs family. In 1943 it ceased working and a tractor was used to provide power for the pump until an electric pump was installed in 1945. The almost daily task of clearing weed from the pump now fell to the Borrett family of Eastfield Farm. The redundant brick tower mill was demolished about 1955 by the Drainage Board who considered it unsafe. They blew it up! The dyke that carried the water from the mill, and later the electric pump, across the Brayden marshes to the Cut continued to be referred to by Gerald and his colleagues as Gibbs Outlet, even though it had been decades since the Gibbs family were there. Paul Borrett of Eastfield Farm was unaware that the dyke from the pump was known as Gibbs outlet. It is surprising how quickly local names get forgotten, though not by Gerald. To him it was always Gibbs outlet, and he calls it that throughout the diary. In 1987 the part of Gibbs outlet that ran directly across Brayden itself was diverted round the top of these marshes by Anglian Water.

Gerald owned a flat-bottomed rectangular boat or pontoon with an outboard motor for moving the reed and sedge about. He called it the 'Black Pig'. He kept this in the Back Dyke at Hickling, which was behind the *Pleasure Boat Inn*, a place where he also stored reed awaiting collection on the public staithe as it was then.

Gerald and his colleagues got round to the marshes mainly by boat. They were self-employed, their own masters as it were, cutting and selling when they had customers. When getting reed or sedge they had to pay rent to the lease holder or owners of the marshes they worked - such as John Buxton at Horsey Hall or the Norfolk Naturalists Trust.

Gerald mostly worked with George Newman, known as 'Newks', who lived at The Green in Hickling, not far from Gerald, and possessed a small motor van to get about. George was a keen footballer, and played for the village Football Club. He continued playing until he was fifty years old. George and Gerald often helped out with jobs around the village, such as tidying up the churchyard at Hickling. George sometimes worked with local thatcher Jack Aldred of Sutton who remembered cutting reed with a scythe: "on a good day Newks and I mowed, dressed, and tied 110-120 bunches a day."

Gerald and George, and their marsh colleagues, their lives dictated by the changing seasons, loved the work on the wide open spaces of rich growth, slads, dykes, drains and marshes, and what they saw there day by day.

Gerald Nudd cutting sedge amongst green reed wearing
thick gloves to protect himself from the sharp saw-sedge.

There were still coypus about in the 1980s and Gerald saw some and where they had been working. These large rat-like creatures spread across Broadland after a few escaped from a fur farm in 1937. Ted Ellis, the well known naturalist, said "In the 1940s they spread to all the Norfolk Broads and gradually into the neighbouring counties of Suffolk and Lincolnshire. They built up a vast population, where there had been hundreds there became thousands, and they reached the point when there were hundreds of thousands."

Taking sedge up Back Dyke to unload onto the public staithe at Hickling.
On top of the sedge is Gerald's bicycle – he called it his Mare of Steel.

Gerald in the Black Pig *as he called it, heading from Hickling Staithe to the sedge marshes.*

The coypu had an impact on Broadland. They tunnelled into the river and dyke banks and threatened the drainage system. They ate farmer's kale and sugar beet. It was said that four coypu could eat the same amount of grass as one sheep, and this was one of the reasons farmers and land owners began to demand some action to control their numbers.

The Ministry of Agriculture, Fisheries and Food (MAFF) at Sprowston Hall just outside Norwich had begun investigating the problem in 1958, and set up the Anti-Coypu Campaign with surveys and systematic trapping. Wire cages three feet long, baited with carrot, sugar beet or fodder beet, caught thousands of these creatures. "We caught thirty-two thousand coypu in nine months" said one operator.

Many of the Hickling marshmen came across the coypu when working the marshes. Gerald reported on 16th March 1983 "Coypus spent the summer in the reed we are cutting now." These creatures were not supposedly extinct until 1989 when coypu trapping was terminated.

There are many references in the diaries to the Common Crane. These large birds once bred in Norfolk around 300 years previously. They returned in September 1979 when John Buxton was informed by Frank Starling, who rented some marshes, that he "had just seen the biggest bloody herons I have ever seen in my life." This pair of Cranes had taken up residence in the Horsey area, and Gerald Nudd, George Newman, Jack Aldred, and other men working on the marshes had seen them, as had the warden of Hickling Broad, Stuart Linsell.

The Cranes arrival and whereabouts was kept secret at first, only locals knowing about them and where they were. Gerald Nudd began his diary in 1980: "Wednesday January 2nd. Wind NW, snow showers. Reed cutting Horsey gap. Several Golden Plovers. Cranes still at Horsey."

The cranes nested in 1981. There were a few set-backs to the pair attempting to raise a family - eggs lost due to flooding, a hatched chick taken by a predator - until 1982 when the first young Crane made it through, eventually becoming "part of a key pair of Broadland cranes for producing young" said John Buxton in *The Norfolk Cranes' Story* [2011]. Other Cranes soon arrived in the area. Gerald, who often, wrongly, called them Crown Cranes, records every time he saw or heard one, and even when he didn't - "No crane sightings today" he would write.

Gerald knew his birds, even down to the smallest that he saw and found in the reeds and sedge, and all the other creatures that inhabited the marshes - caterpillars, butterflies, moths, crayfish. He always did his best for them. If he was worried about the survival of bird's eggs or youngsters, he would move the whole nest to a safer place, hoping the parents would return - which they normally did. "Friday June 29th [1984]. Wind fresh westerly cloudy at times some sunny intervals. Cool. Found another reed buntings nest moved it into a bush newly grown over with sed [sedge]. I hope they return. Swallowtails about. A few dragonflies. No horseflies thank heaven"

The birds on the marshes got used to the men as they worked, sometimes coming quite close. They only became wary if the cutters, or other people, stopped and stared at them. "Saturday 31st July [1980]. Breydon. Wind variable light showers sunny later very warm. Crane family this morning come out of the dyke and lurked along the newly worked up marshes. Later they were in the corn near gibbs outlet. Harrier family were on the wing. I think they are trying to learn him to defend her his self. He come and sat in a bush ten yards away. Several butterflies about found a few eyed hawk moth caterpillars on some goosegrass."

The daily tasks of cutting reed or sedge involved often working in water - he kept a detailed record of the levels. Gerald cut the reeds with a scythe - one of the last of the marshmen to do so - and sedge as well.

The cut reed was picked up and handled into a manageable bunch or bundle by measuring round by hand between forefinger and thumb 2½ times, then combing to get the loose bits out of the bottom of the bundle, so that it could then be 'boarded down' – thumped onto a board so the end was even and neat. The bundle was tied with a bond - usually twine. Each man would cut somewhere around 40 to 70 bundles a day depending on the reed, conditions, water levels etc. The tied bundles were then carried and carted to a nearby staithe and stacked ready for the thatchers or dealers who bought it.

In the summer months it was sedge work. Gerald and George's day often started early not long after dawn so that they could get the sedge work done before it got too hot. In the glare of the summer sun the hard physical work could affect a person. On 18th June 1986 the heat was too much for Billy Nicholls. It made him ill. "Billy Nicholls has sunstroke" recorded Gerald.

Collecting the sedge could be a hazardous occupation, for it had sharp edges and was best handled with gloves. More than once Gerald got cut by the knife-like edges of the saw-sedge leaves. It was handled loose to begin with, and then tied into a bunch about 26 to 28 inches in diameter. Bunches of sedge were never quite as neat at the bottom as bundles of reed. The sedge was then loaded into Gerald's flat bottom boat and taken to one of the staithes where it was heaped to dry and be ready for collection. Reed was fine for the main thatch, the sedge being used for the ridge as it bent easily over the top and formed a convenient capping. Reed was cut once a year

George 'Newks' Newman with Gerald moving a workboat loaded with sedge in Catfield Dyke on 2nd September 1982.

while sedge ground had to be left two or three years between each cutting for it to grow. Often sedge was mixed with growing reed and had to be sorted.

By starting work early Gerald and George might be finished by lunchtime or early afternoon, and often Gerald would bicycle back to Hickling to the *Pleasure Boat Inn* for a spot of lunch. He might also call in at the *Greyhound* on his way home as well where he was always welcome. In fact if people saw his bike propped up outside they would go in and enjoy his company. Once a week Gerald put on his best clothes and went there for a Crib [cribbage – card game] night.

Nearly everyone in the district knew Gerald. He was friendly and popular. Hazel Nudd, the wife of local farm worker Harry Nudd, remembers. "I met Gerald and his brother Austin soon after I moved to Hickling in 1973. They were both single and lived with their parents in a council house on 'The Track' as it was locally known. I got to know Gerald better after I married his second cousin Harry Nudd in 1977. I recall Gerald as a tough, hard working man, out on the marshes in all weathers cutting reed and sedge, and with a love of the local landscape and wildlife.

"He was a sociable person who enjoyed meeting his friends in the village pubs and could always be relied upon to tell a good story of local life. Underneath he was a caring man often showing concern for his younger brother Austin who had health problems. There are many people who knew Gerald better and for longer than me but he was the sort of person who made friends easily and left a lasting impression on his many acquaintances."

Local family names pop up in the diary from time to time, such as the name Perry. This was Mrs. Perry who had Poplar Farm, later taken over by her son James Perry, who also had some fields and marshes near Stubb Mill, and who occasionally employed Gerald Nudd when other work was slack, such as helping with the pea harvest or loading sugar beet. James recalls: "Gerald was one of the last to cut reed and sedge by hand, carrying it off the marsh and stacking ready to sell. I wonder how many roofs and ridges Gerald had cut reed in the winter months for and sedge in the summer. He started early in the morning in the summer months on the sedge to get it done before it was too hot, and those bloody horseflies started to bite.

"Gerald had a quick eye for nature. He would work round a harrier or bitterns nest so not to disturb it. He knew more about the marsh and birds than a lot of well educated people. He enjoyed telling people about nature. I was on a boat at Hickling when he said 'Did you see that'? I expected to see a wind surfer falling off his board. 'No, there' he said. It was a grass snake swimming past the boat with its head just out of the water. I never saw it but he did, and he shared it with us."

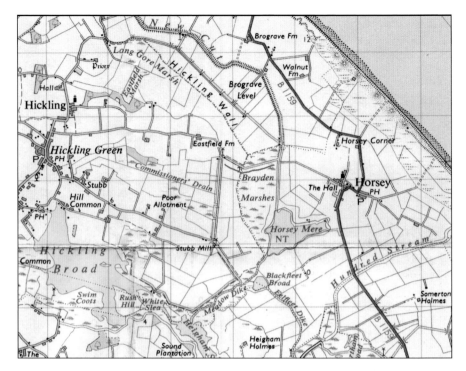

A 1954 map of the Hickling and Horsey area where Gerald Nudd worked as a marshman in the 1980s. Note the dyke, underlined in red, which took water from the electric pump, formerly from a drainage mill, near Eastfield Farm, across Brayden Marshes to Waxham Cut. This was known as Gibbs outlet after the Gibbs family who had once looked after the drainage mill. In 1987 the part of Gibbs outlet which went across Brayden itself was diverted to the north of these marshes when a new channel was constructed by Anglian Water Authority to help reduce the amount of ochre being carried into Waxham Cut.

Gibbs outlet took water from Eastfield drainage pump to Brayden marshes in the distance, then across to Waxham Cut. In 1987 the part of the outlet across Braydon was dammed off and the water diverted around the top of Brayden marshes to the Cut.

The electric drainage pump at Eastfield. This sent water from the marshes behind Eastfield farm and between that and Stubb Mill, down Gibbs outlet and across Brayden marshes to Waxham Cut. Note the rake which automatically does the job of weed clearing.

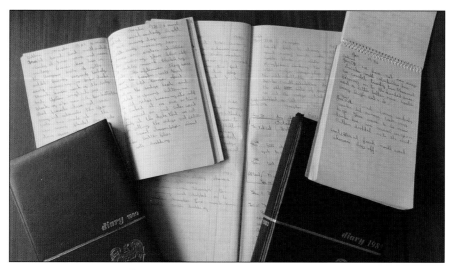

The diaries of Gerald Nudd - from 1980 to 1986.

The Man and his Diaries

The diary begins on Tuesday 1st January 1980. The entry for that day says simply "Wind north west. Snow showers. Holiday." So no work that day. On Wednesday 2nd he began "Reed cutting Horsey Gap. Several Golden plovers cranes still at Horsey." The next day: "Thursday 3rd January. Hard frost snowed later turning to rain Wind SE." On "Friday 4th January. Rain and drizle first part of morning cleared later from the west. Finished holly pond back of Horsey Hall. To much water back of hills. Saw one cock stonechat Horsey Gap. Crown cranes still at Horsey."

On the marshes he was often working in water, and the height was important to him. If there was too much he would not be able to cut. Depending on the level, and getting to the site, he wore short rubber boots or longer waders. At times the tops of the waders were folded down to just below the knee for more comfortable working. On Saturday 5th January he bought a new pair of waders, they cost him £22.50. He finished cutting at Horsey Gap on Monday 7th January with "180 Bunches good reed." The next day "Wind easterly cold odd hail shower in morning. Started cutting on Horsey Marsh better reed 45 bunches. Mowed for others."

The diary entries began with the date followed by the weather and what he saw. The words just flowed from his mind through his ball-point pen onto the paper. "Thursday 10th January. Wind east to south east. Cold sleet showers. Finished first part of one marsh. Aproximatly six hundred bunches. Barnacle Geese and white fronted Geese at Mere farm [on the marshes behind Horsey Mere between the B1159 coast road and Blackfleet Broad] arrived today odd redshank. I [one] Marsh harrier one or two medow pipits feeding with us."

As mentioned, Gerald preferred to use a scythe when cutting reed, cutting with a swing of the blade with his body following through, a perfect rhythm and movement obtained after much practice making it look easy to the onlooker. Actually it was hard work. Gerald's scythe had a wild rose briar hoop fitted at the back which helped sweep the cut reed into a swathe so that it lay down on the ground with the base of the reeds together, making it easy to pick up. "Wednesday 9th January. Good days work 40 bunches not bad reed. Wind east at first went south east later. Saw four bearded tits, one stonechat dozen Hooper [Whooper] swans. Broke end of scythe." His writing was to the point. "Friday 11th January. Dentist. Wind west. Fine day."

Even in the cold of winter birds were about and Gerald was always watching them and what they were up to. "Thursday 24th January. Wind westerly. Sunny later early morning frost ice on the reed for an hour or two. Cock hen harrier came within ten yards of us near Cubbits marsh. One bearded tit. No geese today, one or two magpies about the first we have seen for weeks. Reed very tall first time for several years probably due to the use of scythes. 40."

The next day he noticed that "Pheasants are getting braver probably due to the near end of the shooting season." "Friday 1ST February. Wind northerly cool sunny day. One pheasant keeps feeding with us very tame, looks like one from Burnly Hall estate [farm and marsh at Somerton] released earlier on in the shooting season. No stonechats so far one Barn owl first thing this morning."

Reed cutting went on throughout the winter. He recorded on Friday 25 January 1980 that "Reed has improved greatly on the Marsh next to Cubbits Marsh rather tall and straight especially where we cleared up two years ago." The many bundles of reed were carried off the marsh on the shoulder

Gerald with the Mayfield motorised mower here being used
to carry bundles of sedge and pull a loaded sledge.

though sometimes Gerald records that "Sledged most of the reed out at Starchgrass end today" using a Mayfield motor mower. Mostly the bundles were then loaded onto a boat to be taken to a staithe where they were stacked. For this water transport Gerald and George Newman used pontoons. "Monday 25th February. Rained nearly all day and foggy at times. Moved Pontoons from Potterheigham to Waxham cut and picked the other one up and took them all to Breydon."

For the sedge Gerald normally scythed or occasionally used the Mayfield tractor mower. This consisted of a petrol driven engine mounted on a two-wheeled frame with long handles for the operator who walked behind. This particular machine was fitted on the front with a reciprocating sharp knife and tines, so that Gerald simply steered the machine into the sedge to be cut, or attached a rope to the back to tow a loaded sledge out of the marsh. The Mayfield was fitted with extra wide wheels to stop it sinking into the soft marsh and leaving tracks behind.

Left to right George Newman, Gerald Nudd and Billy Nicholls
taking sedge to Somerton Staithe on Richard Starling's pontoon.

Gerald noticed everything around him. "Friday 7th March 1980. Evidence of Otters on the west side of the mere fish trimed out. Started clearing the slads for John Buxton." He uses the term slad many times in the diaries. Richard Starling, who had been working the marshes around Martham Broad, and knew Gerald quite well, described slad as 'a shallow flooded area'. It is an old Norfolk word which no one now appears to use - 'scrape' is often used instead. According to Walter Rye's *A Glossary of Words Used in East Anglia* [1895] slad or slade means 'a narrow slip of boggy ground'.

On Friday 4th April Gerald records seeing "very large pike spawning in the dyke to Breydon accompanied by jacks [young pike] about four pounds each. Crown cranes flew across the mere on to the Somerton marshes."

Sometimes the weather made life difficult. "Tuesday 18th March. East fresh at first misty light drizzle. Made up to gale force made reedcutting a bit difficult. A pair of oyster catchers kicking up a racket considering its cold enough to snow."

"Wednesday 19th March. Wind north east strong cold sunny periods odd showers. no work to windy. Mended an old scythe."

"Wednesday 16th April. Brought Perrys fordson major [tractor] around to Michael Brooks [local engineer and lorry driver] for repair. Mayfield broke down."

" Friday 18th April. Brian [Applegate] heard the cuckoo…George saw an eel." A few days later Gerald "Saw a mungjack deer in the sedge"

"Tuesday 6th May. Boating up Horsey mere holed pontoon pulled her out at Waxham for repair…A pair of swans at the staithe with eight cygnets."

"Wednesday 7th May. moved sedge from Waxham cut to Tom Lings [farmer south of Hickling Broad] cleared the last few bunches off Horsey… water a very dirty colour in Waxham cut. …Should start getting Toms reed out tomorrow."

"Saturday 10th May. scrubbed the bottom of the pontoon." The next day, a Sunday, "started painting the pontoon."

Gerald, wearing folded down waders, on a work punt.

"Tuesday 27th May. Started sedge cutting along side of Gibbs outlet. Water very low with rust coming off the bottom forming a nasty slick of scum on the surface lovely roach dead primesium on Hickling. [prymnesium parvum - an alga which grows in brackish water producing a toxin which kills fish]. Found one bitterns nest four eggs. The eggs had been got at by crows or something such a pity. We saw the first swallow tail butterfly today. The sedge is very dry at the moment with a lot of last years seed stalks in it. one harrier working the rusty marsh for several minutes."

The reference to rust is part of the red coloured run off out of the dykes near Waxham Cut. Richard Starling said "The orange coloured water (ochre) was caused by the chemical reaction in the drainage ditches on surrounding arable land as water levels were lowered. The lowering of water levels enabled arable farming but his caused 'ochre' water to be discharged into the Broads system via pumps."

"Tuesday 10th June…scum on the water. A few lillies coming out marvellous how they come out at all with all that rusty scum on the surface. We mowed a sedge warblers nest up unfortunately but moved it to some thick sedge lets hope they go back."

"Wednesday 11th June. The sedge warblers have gone back to the nest after we moved it yesterday." "Thursday 19th June. ..The sedge warbler we moved has hatched with three young."

Another aid was a tractor Gerald and George bought. "Friday 20th June….Used the big tractor for the first time we had to be very careful." "Saturday 21st June. Paid for the tractor. Lennie More has bought Mrs. Pratts old cottage."

"Thursday 26th June. …Scum in the outlet coming up off the bottom due to heat of the day. They have been pumping at Eastfield for the last four days more pollution." "Monday 30th June…Snipe drumming for half the day….Some of the water lillies are dying I do not think they like the rust. Two dead eels towards eastfield pump. Scum very thick on top of the water near the pontoon." "Friday 4th July. Believed we saw an osprey today coming on to the mere and crossing towards Hickling."

"Tuesday 15th July. Mowed on to a sedge warblers nest four eggs." "Wednesday 16th July. Another sedge warblers nest five eggs. We think she will stay by it." "Wednesday 30th July sedge warblers have hatched out. And we found a eyed hawkmoth caterpillar making his way to chrisaliss."

"Tuesday 2nd September. the yacht Butterfly returned back to her usual berth at the mouth of Gibbs outlet." "Tuesday 9th September. Josh Nudds funeral Gorleston" [an uncle]. "Friday 26th September. a lot of swallows and martins on the telephone wires first thing this morning on Hickling Green. There seems to be a good breeding season for the wrens this year."

"Monday 29th September. A merlin passed through this lunchtime. Mushrooms have still got the maggot." "Thursday 9th October. boated all the sedge up today." "Wednesday 15th October. Crown cranes flew across on to Ellisses Marshes [Ellis - local farmer] and four about an hour made a hell of a din. One buzard gliding on a thermal being mobbed by gulls he did not seem at all bothered. One or two bearded tits about. Cygnets on the wing with the old gal." "Friday 17th October. No work very wet."

"Monday 20th October. Water very high. The highest we have seen for some years. Unable to cut had to pack up." The weather was against them for several days and the water was too high to work. It was not until "Thursday 30th October. Water has started to drop." "Monday 3rd

November. Water has dropped the lowest for years ebbing this morning. We moved the tractor off the marsh to Eastfield pump. Crown cranes feeding in the dry marsh first time we have seen them in the sedge bed."

A week later still working on the sedge. "Tuesday 11th November. Loading sedge." "Wednesday 12th November. Boated all the sedge up to Horsey Mill." Soon the reed would be ready to cut, and he kept an eye on the situation. "Monday 24th November. Leaf nearly off the reed early this year. Mushrooms still growing on the marshes." "Friday 28th November. Very rough day north west gale force heavy rain and snow at times went eel fishing, one pike four pounds, eel and an unknown fish." "Monday 1st December. Started reedcutting Blackfleet broad. 70. One cruiser came up Meadow dyke [connecting Horsey Mere to Heigham Sound] this dinnertime must have been a honeymoon couple, how cold the weather is." "Wednesday 10th December. My uncle J L Nudd [Jack Nudd] died this morning at North Walsham Hospital he was 71." And so the cycle of marsh life and human life continued.

Gerald Nudd relaxing in the Pleasure Boat Inn *at Hickling. On Gerald's left are Harry and Hazel Nudd.*

Now we will look at one complete year [the day, date and month have been regularised – from then on each entry is as Gerald wrote it] as Gerald recorded it in his diary of 1983. The first day of January, a Saturday, it seems he had a day off. On the Sunday he went for a day's sea fishing a couple of miles up the Norfolk coast off Castle Farm above Sea Palling. On Tuesday 4th January he was back at work cutting and carting reeds.

Left to right Gerald Nudd, Billy Nicholls, George Newman and Richard Starling leaning on fork. Somerton drainage mill is in the background. This photograph was taken on Cadbury's sedge bed at Martham Broad in October 1984.

A Year from the Gerald Nudd Diaries
1983

Saturday 1st January. Wind southwesterly fine mild.

Sunday 2nd January. Wind south west fresh mild. A few northern divers on the sea. Odd guillemot. One or two geese passing through caught about thirty whiting on the long lines.

Monday 3rd January. Wind strong to gale southwest. Fine at first rained later. To rough to go to sea.

Tuesday 4th January. Wind south west to west gale force sunny at times wind eased later. Marsh harriers about several ducks in the slad mere farm. Several teal. No crane sightings.

Wednesday 5th January. Cloudy at first sunny later wind fresh westerly gale force early evening. Three hoopers [whooper] swans flew over not many in this area this year. Shelducks about. No signs of the stonechats as yet. Two frogs in the reed seem quite active. No crane sightings.

Thursday 6th January. Wind strong to gale south west cloudy at times rained early afternoon. One marsh harrier came right up to us when we were sheltering under a bale of reed mere farm. Several ducks on the move today. Aunt Celia passed on.

[This was Joshua Nudds widow, Amy Cecelia Nudd, who died on 31st December 1982]

Friday 7th January. Wind strong south west colder. Day off went to Aunt Celia's funeral.

Saturday 8th January. Wind fresh south west nice sunny day. Mild.

Sunday 9th January. Cloudy start sunny later wind fresh to strong south westerly.

Monday 10th January. Mere Farm. Cloudy start wind fresh south westerly a very light shower. Mild. Odd bunch of geese going over. Several duck in the wet marsh. Marsh harriers about. No crane sighting.

Stonechat by Roger Nudd.

Tuesday 11th January. Wind fresh westerly mild fresh. Lone hooper swan flew over. No crane sighting or stonechat. Mute swans in the slad.

Wednesday 12th January. Wind fresh south westerly sunny periods. Not many pheasants about this year must have been a poor breeding season due to the wet early summer. Marsh harrier working Cubbits marsh. Barn owl working mere farm marshes this afternoon. No crane sightings. A few small drinker moth caterpillars in the marsh starchgrass end.

Thursday 13th January. ½ day. Early morning rain.

Friday 14th January. Day off. Early morning snow turned to rain.

Saturday 15th January. Fine and sunny wind strong west to north west.

Sunday 16th January. Fine and sunny wind strong north west.

Monday 17th January. Mere Farm. Cloudy at times some sunshine. Wind strong westerly mild. Water has made up driving us out of the Duck pond to Cubbits marsh better reed. One hen harrier Horsey corner. Several golden plover about. No bittern sightings or cranes. Two marsh harriers working mere farm marshes. No signs of any stonechats this year.

Tuesday 18th January. Mere Farm. Wind north west strong showers in the afternoon cold.

Wednesday 19th January. Mere Farm. Wind strong to gale north west showers at times sleet and rain. One Bittern flew out of the reed marsh near steam mill corner [between the Horsey Road and Martham Broad]. Cranes come through twice today. Ducks very restless flying out of the slad and on to the mere several times.

Thursday 20th January. Wind fresh westerly hazy sunshine cold. Water very high on the marshes starchgrass end. Looks if it is coming through the wall there.

Friday 21st January. Mere Farm. Wind fresh westerly sunny a little milder. Marshes still flooded down near starchgrass. Tractored out one load . Then moved the new stacks out. One lone crane came over us and turned away.

Saturday 22nd January. Wind south west fresh at times cloudy but mild. One or two seals about geese flying along the coast. Went herring catching. About two hundred some sprats several nice herring. [Tim Cox had a smoke house].

Sunday 23rd January. Castle Farm Eccles. Wind fresh southerly. Unable to go fishing shipped a big sea going off. Water very thick plenty of herring there.

Monday 24th January. Mere Farm. Wind fresh southerly cloudy rained after miday mild. Cranes calling on Martham holms. Harriers working the reedbeds. Several drinker moth caterpillars on Cubitts marsh. Grey squirell on the road near Castles plantation just before Priory farm Hickling.

Tuesday 25th January. Mere Farm. Wind light to fresh south westerly cloudy at times very mild. Cranes calling this morning on Martham holms for quite some time. Harriers about. More pheasants showing themselves now perhaps they realise shooting is nearly finished.

Wednesday 26th January. Mere Farm. Wind light south west very mild sunny all day but towards late afternoon clouded over. Cranes calling on Martham holms this morning. About forty hooper swans flew over. Odd wader passing through. Finished off Cubbitts marsh today.

Thursday 27th January. Mere Farm. Wind fresh to strong south west to west sunny periods. Several lapwings near starchgrass. A few golden plovers. Marsh harriers working the reed marshes. Barn owl hunting as we left off this afternoon. One or two nice flocks of pigeons about.

Friday 28th January. Mere farm. Rain and showers sunny periods. Wind fresh westerly.

Saturday 29th January. Wind fresh to strong westerly sunny day cooler.

Sunday 30th January. Wind westerly fresh to strong sunny periods cooler.

Monday 31st January. Mere Farm. Wind variable first thing made up later strong wigeon and teal shovelers and mallard in the wet marsh. Pheasant getting bolder on the last day of shooting.

Tuesday 1st February. Mere farm. Wind south west to west gale to storm force. Showers in the afternoon. Water very high flood warnings on the coast.

Teal by Roger Nudd.

Wednesday 2nd February. Mere farm. Wind light southerly to west fine sunny day cool. Several pheasants calling on the marshes. Several ducks about and golden plover. A score of hoopers on the marshes other side of mere farm marshes. Odd meadow pipit on the reed grounds.

Thursday 3rd February. Wind fresh northerly sunny periods showers first thing cold. Cranes passed through this morning three. Harriers working the reed grounds. A few more pigeons getting about. One or two cormorants flying over.

Friday 4th February. Mere farm. Wind fresh southerly nice sunny day cold after overnight frost cloud coming in towards dusk with freshening winds. Several geese on Martham holms. Pink feet and Canada. About five coypus went into the reeds in a stretch from Blackfleet to the top of the sounds [Heigham Sound]. Two or three harriers working the reedbeds. Water has dropped a little.

Saturday 5th February. Fine and sunny wind northerly cold. Showers later.

Sunday 6th February. Sunny periods and sleet showers wind northerly cold.
Mrs Mirtle Nudd died at Stubbs Mill. [Myrtle Nudd 1912-1983, William Nudd's wife]

Monday 7th February. Mere Farm. Wind north easterly cold sunny periods and sleet showers. Water has dropped a bit. Several Canada geese came on to the mere this afternoon. Several wigeon and other duck in the wet marsh. And a nice lot of coots. No crane sightings today.

Tuesday 8th February. Horsey Mere Shaws Boathouse. Wind north east fresh to strong snow showers. Cold. Water dropping. The barn owl was working the marshes very late this morning. Marsh harries about. Moved out on to the edge of the mere. Water dropping.

Wednesday 9th February. Shaws Boathouse. The mere. Wind north east fresh snow showers cold. Water still dropping. One marsh harrier working Denes Farm Sea Palling. Reports of a white tailed sea eagle in the Fleggburgh area in the last few days.

Thursday 10th February. Horsey Mere. Wind variable at first veered westerly light snow showers. Snowed heavier late afternoon.

Friday 11th February. Wind strong north east dropped to light variable snow showers cold.

Saturday 12th February. Fine and sunny very cold wind north east fresh.

Sunday 13th February. Wind north east fresh sunny at times cold.

Monday 14th February. Wind fresh to strong northeasterly sunny morning cloudy afternoon. Very cold freezing all day. (Went to Mrs Mirtle Nudds funeral Hickling Church).

Tuesday 15th February. Shaws Boathouse. Wind fresh to strong north easterly cold sunny periods. Water still low. A few coots this end two or three swans. No cranes about. Three twitchers [bird watchers] came along the wall this afternoon.

Wednesday 16th February. Wind fresh easterly sunny day cold. Water low. One lone marsh harrier working the woods near the hall [Horsey Hall]. One woodcock rose out of the bracken this morning. Crane calling on the marshes back of the hall.

Thursday 17th February. Wind easterly fresh cloudy morning sunny afternoon cold.

Friday 18th February. The mere summer house. Wind south east fresh sunny day cold. Lone marsh harrier hawking the marshes. One bearded tit in the tall reeds.

Saturday 19th February. Sutton Slushy loke. Wind light south easterly. Cloudy and cool. Went to Sutton high fen and helped Tony Patterson [local gamekeeper] to cut John Withers reed. One lone harrier working the fen. A few bullfinches and chaffinches about. The reed was fairly good apart from sedge tussocks and old sallow reeds due to John Withers excessive burning over the years. Could be a bunch or two of sedge if he was not so match happy. [John Withers was a farmer at Sutton, also chairman of the Smallburgh and District Drainage Board].

Sunday 20th February. Castle Farm Eccles. Went sea fishing not much doing. Three codling dozen whitings one dab and fourteen herring. Wind northeasterly fresh rain showers four o'clock time.

Monday 21st February. Horsey mere. Wind fresh easterly cloudy cold. Swans fighting on the mere for their territorys. Still a lot of ducks resting on the mere no crane sightings.

Tuesday 22nd February. Horsey mere. Wind strong to gale south east sunny day but cold. Bittern has been sleeping in the reed near the summer house. Large pile of droppings. Water very low. Cormorants still fishing the mere. George saw a bittern near the summer house.

Wednesday 23rd February. South side of mere. Wind south east fresh to strong sunny but cold. Several bunches of wigeon resting steam mill corner and foreign mallard. One buzzard working the woods back of the hall. One sparrow hawk along the Waxham sea Palling road.

Thursday 24th February. South side of mere. Wind south east fresh sunny morning cloudy later a bit milder. Wigeon chasing about today. They seem to have got the spring feeling. Eight drakes seem to be chasing one duck in the air. Perhaps a sign of milder weather. Water very low. The lowest we have seen it for some years.

Friday 25th February. Blackfleet [Broad] Robin [Myhill] mere. Wind light to fresh south easterly. Misty day cloudy. One marsh harrier chasing the ducks in the broad. Water very low.

Saturday 26th February. Palling gap. Wind light to fresh south westerly, mild rain and drizzle at first misty, sunny late afternoon. Went linging and herring catching. 25 codling off 200 hooks [long line with baited hooks]. 25 herring some full. One or two redthroated divers about odd guillemot. A few geese brent. Several lapwings coming in off the sea.

Sunday 27th February. Wind fresh west nor west, rain at first fine and sunny later. Mild. Went down to Eccles and Sea Palling to see if it was any good. Some boats off after herring. But decided against it.

Monday 28th February. Blackfleet Broad. Wind fresh to strong west veering north west at times sunny day cool showers late afternoon. Redshanks calling in blackfleet several duck here one pair of swans. One frog stirredhimself this morning yellow.

Hen Harrier by Roger Nudd.

Tuesday 1st March. Blackfleet Broad. Wind fresh northerly cloudy at times odd sunny periods cool. Water making up. Redshanks calling. Cranes making a lot of noise in Breydon [Brayden marshes next to Horsey Mere and Waxham Cut]. Harriers working motley marshes on the way home. One hen harrier came right over the green low and flew on to the fields. People did not seem to worry him to much or houses. One mad march hare near Billy Nudds wall this morning [William Nudd of Stubb Mill]. Two coursers went through. [Cream Coloured Courser - a rare wader]

Wednesday 2nd March. Blackfleet. Wind fresh south west cool sunny periods. Water holding its own coots calling in blackfleet spring seems on its way.

Thursday 3rd March. Day off. Wind southerly fresh rain at times cool. We went sea fishing longline 200 hooks one dozen small codling. Lapwings coming in off the sea.

Friday 4th March. Mere Farm. Wind fresh easterly rained miday sunny later in the afternoon. George ['Newks' Newman] found a rails nest just built.

Saturday 5th March. Mere farm. Wind fresh westerly sunny periods. To rough to go fishing.

Sunday 6th March. Wind fresh westerly nice sunny day. Mild. To rough to go fishing.

Monday 7th March. Blackfleet Broad. Wind light westerly sunny at times very mild. Water has made up. Bittern trying to boom near Meadow dyke. One or two frogs moving about now. Water beatles moving about now several insects about today very mild miday. A pair of marsh harriers quartering Breydon. Birds calling today perhaps spring is on the way.

Tuesday 8th March. Blackfeet Broad. Wind fresh south westerly fine sunny day. Mild. A bittern flew out of Blackfleet and landed in steam mill corner today. About a score of hoopers on the mere. Redshanks calling in the slad. Lone Bumble bee just out. Lapwings doing courtship flying. Water has dropped again.

Wednesday 9th March. Blackfleet Broad. Wind westerly fresh at times, sunny day mild. Two bitterns booming in Blackfleet slad this morning.   And later on. Harriers about. No crane sightings. Colt starting to move now.

Thursday 10th March. Mere Farm Horsey. Wind fresh westerly fine sunny day mild. Water has made up a bit. Bittern flew from starchgrass to meadow dyke. One lone sparrow hawk working the marshes. A few waders in the wet marsh . Golden plover and ringed plover we passed close by. They were not bothered by us. Proving the experts wrong again.

Friday 11th March. Blackfleet Broad. Wind fresh easterly cloudy day cooler. Bittern still booming in blackfeet slad. Redshanks calling now and then. A pair of mute swans in Blackfleet nesting. There seem to be a few more magpies and jays about nowerdays. Water has lifted a little.

Saturday 12th March. Whiteslea. Hickling marshes. Wind fresh southerly cloudy start sunnier cooler. Several pigeons feeding on Perry's corn. A flock of reed buntings as well. Golden plover going through. One Bunch had a few starling flying with them. Three cranes come towards us gliding then veered off to Martham holms. Cut several bunches of reed for Mrs Perry.

Sunday 13th March. Hickling. Wind south east fine sunny day. Cooler.

Monday 14th March. Blackfleet & Brograve marsh. Wind fresh south westerly sunny periods showers in the afternoon. One dead jack pike in one of the holes looks if he got a dose of marsh gas. Redshanks about. A lot of pigeons on the marshes at horsey. Arrived this afternoon at Brograve marsh. One lone crane flew across and the other three cranes in the sedge bed kicked up a lot of noise. He flew on to Waxham level out of the way. A few minutes later they flew off to the back of the hall. The reed has come back on this marsh very tall and fairly thick. Last time we cut it was ten years ago George and myself. Although the bottom is bad for getting about.

Tuesday 15th March. Brograve marsh. Wind easterly veering northerly fresh. Overnight frost fine sunny day. No cranes today. Harrier working the Waxham level. Several drinker moth caterpillars in the tall reeds we are cutting here. Good reed the best we have cut on Horsey estate for years. The bottom is very bad for getting about.

Wednesday 16th March. Brograve marsh. Wind fresh south westerly sunny morning clouded over later with some rain mild. Coypus spent the summer in the reed we are cutting now. Rails calling in the sedge. Kestrel playing about near the mill. They always have a nest there. We found some old cockle shells where they dredged the spoil out two years ago.

Thursday 17th March. Brograve marsh. Wind westerly fresh sunny periods rained in the afternoon mild. Water making up a bit. Bittern booming in this marsh. Bearded tits calling in the tall reeds. Crane making a lot of noise this afternoon. Two flew out of their breeding ground leaving one in our marsh. No butterflies as yet one or two bees about. Frogs on the move now.

Friday 18th March. Brograve marsh. Wind westerly fresh sunny periods cloudy at times mild. Water holding down. Harriers working the sedge bed. Cranes calling in Breydon. Bittern booming below us we disturbed him in the short sedge on the way home. Reed bunting calling for mates. One hen stonechat in borrets loke [Paul Borrett of Eastfield farm] on the way home. The first time we have seen one for a very long time.

Saturday 19th March. Perry's marsh. Wind south westerly veered north west later cooler.

Sunday 20th March. Wind fresh south westerly some rain . Rained later.

Monday 21st March. Brograve marsh. Wind south west at first freshened westerly cooler heavy showers rain and sleet in the afternoon. Water still holding down.

Tuesday 22nd March. Horsey. Wind strong to gale westerly showers late afternoon cold. One lone swallow flew over the green and stayed a few seconds. Went down mere farm and tydied up the reed which Aldred had pulled about.

Wednesday 23rd March. Brograve marsh. Wind southerly fresh to strong rain at times heavy midelmorning cold. Packed up and went home again. Water up a bit.

Thursday 24th March. Brograve marsh. Wind strong to gale northerly colder. Some showers good sunny intervals. Bittern booming a few yards from me several times. Meadow pipit feeding on the reed stubble. Bearded tits about. No crane sightings. How cold it is the weather must have put them off. Water has not up to much at the moment.

Friday 25th March. Brograve marsh. Wind fresh to strong northerly clouded over later. Rain and showers wind backed southwesterly veered northerly severe gale northerly cold.

Saturday 26th March. Hickling. Wind moderating north west sunny periods cold.

Sunday 27th March. Hickling. Wind northerly fresh sunny periods showers later.

Monday 28th March. Horsey mere. Wind fresh northerly sunny periods heavy showers. Two cranes flew in to Breydon and the other pair flew to the back of the hall. They seem to have split up again. Several pochard on Hickling. Water has made up. But our dam is still holding it out at the pump Brograve end.

Gerald on Brograve Marsh in 1985, carrying bundles of reed.

Tuesday 29th March. Brograve marsh. Wind fresh westerly sunny morning clouded over and rained in the afternoon. Cranes one pair came and dropped in to the area. Bittern booming near us. Water rails calling in the reed in to the marsh. Frogs croaking this morning being a little milder than of late. Going getting rather heavy here now as we get to the end of this marsh reed not so good now quality wise.

Wednesday 30th March. Meadow Dyke end. Wind fresh west south west sunny morning. Showers in the afternoon heavy later. With thunder and lightening. Cranes flying towards Breydon. Bittern booming near steamill corner. Oyster catchers on the wing. Swans seem to have nested on the west side this year.

Thursday 31st March. Wind south west fresh sunny some cloud showers miday and heavy in the afternoon. A little milder. Cranes getting off Motley marshes heading back home. Grebes paired off on the mere. Bittern booming in steamill corner.

Friday 1st April. Perry Hickling Marshes. Wind fresh to strong north east cold. Fine morning showers then rained all afternoon. Crane came along then turned back to Motley marsh. Red shanks feeding in the flooded corn. Ducks sitting about.

Saturday 2nd April. Perry Hickling Marshes. Wind northerly fresh fine day. Cold towards evening. A little milder. Two old hares creeping across the fields. Several pigeons playing Perry's corn. Short eared owl in Perry's marsh. No crane sightings.

Sunday 3rd April. Some light showers fine later cold.

Monday 4th April. Wet morning snow very early turned to rain fine later cold.

Tuesday 5th April. Horsey mere North. Wind fresh southerly sunny morning showery later some heavy hail. And thunder and lightening. Over night fresh cold. Bittern booming up near the summer house. Bearded tits working in the old reed. Cranes calling off and on all morning in the back of Breydon. One dead pike floating in Meadow dyke one large bream last week. I hope prymnesiom [Prymnesium - an algae deadly to fish] has not started again like it did last year about this time.

Wednesday 6th April. Waxham cut. Wind fresh south west sunny morning showers midd afternoon a little warmer. Hen harrier working near the mouth of the cut. Marsh harriers about. No crane sightings. Bittern booming near the summer house.

Marsh Harrier by Roger Nudd.

Thursday 7th April. Waxham cut. Wind fresh south westerly sunny period a little warmer. One lone crane flew on to the Hickling marshes this morning and went back to the hall later. Oyster catchers chasing each other about. Rails call now and then. Marsh harrier working the middle of Breydon. Rooks nesting near Hickling green one nest last year three this year. This has never hapened before.

Friday 8th April. Castle Farm Eccles. Wind fresh to strong south west veering westerly when showers occurred. One or two seals about oyster catchers. Ringed plover. Caught a score of herrings in two shoots weather roughed up coming back and going in. A bit naughty.

Saturday 9th April. J Perry. Hickling marshes. Wind south west veered easterly in the afternoon fine sunny day warmer. One crane on the hundred acre [Hundred Acre Marsh south of Stubb Mill and east of Whiteslea]. Shoverlers chasing the ducks about. Ringed plover on the flooded corn patches. One or two hares about. No signs of any colt on these marshes yet.

Sunday 10th April. Hickling. Heavy rain at times wind south east.

Monday 11th April. Horsey. Wet all day wind afternoon gale force with rain. (One swallow Whiteslea Hickling).

Tuesday 12th April. Horsey. Wind strong to gale northerly heavy showers some sunny periods. One pair of marsh harriers Mere farm. And at Breydon. One lone wheatear north side of the mere. No crane sightings. Water making up. Tydied up the car park at Horsey staithe. To much wind for boating up.

Wednesday 13th April. Horsey mere. Wind fresh westerly sunny period light showers later warmer. About six dadchicks in one lump near the summer house. Harriers working mere farm. And Breydon. And the hundred acre Hickling. One or two peacocks out for an airing today. Robin and blackbird getting worms for their young in the garden this afternoon. Water up a bit boating out.

Thursday 14th April. Horsey mere. Wind fresh westerly fine day some cloud not cold. Water easing. Several magpies nesting in the area. They seem to be on the increase again. Thought we saw a cuckoo at Nudds mill this morning. Boating up reed today. [Nudds Mill now known as Stubb Mill]

Friday 15th April. Horsey Mere Farm. Wind fresh westerly nice sunny day a little warmer. One cuckoo on the wing Stubbs mill. Lone swallow blackfleet broad. Several Black headed gulls in the slad teal shoveler at mere farm. Harriers about. Several butterflies about. Brimstone tortoiseshell and peacocks today. No warblers as yet.

Saturday 16th April. Hickling. Fine sunny day wind fresh southerly warmer.

Sunday 17th April. Hickling. Cloudy outbreaks of rain mild.

Monday 18th April. Hickling. Wind north east strong heavy rain cold.

Tuesday 19th April. Hickling. Wind south westerly rain and showers finer in the afternoon cold.

Wednesday 20th April. Horsey mere. Overnight frost sunny morning clouded over and rained heavy middafternoon cool. One or two swallows and martins about. One or two warblers have arrived. Cuckoos about. Crane flew in to their area this morning. Cutting sedge ahead of the hymac [mechanical digger used to clean out dykes] near the summer house water high.

Thursday 21st April. Horsey mere. Wind fresh southerly sunny at times dry day warmer. Reed and sedge warblers here now. Canadian geese settling in where they have cut a dyke to bank the walls in on the north east side. Water still very high.

Friday 22nd April. Horsey mere. Wind fresh to strong some good sunny period cool. One common tern flew across the mere. Bittern booming in blackfleet. Cranes about. Water has dropped a bit.

Saturday 23rd April. Hickling Perrys Marsh. Wind fresh south east sunny periods warm on the marsh. Shovelers about and oystercatchers ringed plovers feeding on the flooded patches of corn. Yellow wagtails. One or two peacocks on the reed. Cuckoos about. A swift flew over the green this afternoon.

Sunday 24th April. Sunny morning showers later warmer.

Monday 25th April. Horsey mere. Wind fresh easterly cold morning with rain fine miday wind veered south west sunny afternoon warmer. Several harriers about four mere farm. And then in Breydon. Cranes calling down there this morning. Grebes courtship dancing on the mere. Several drinker moth caterpillars this year. Better year for them. Water has dropped.

Tuesday 26th April. Horsey mere. Wind light to fresh south easterly fine sunny day no rain for a change. Harriers about several more warblers now. Have [not] heard the grasshopper warbler as yet. Water has made up a bit on this full moon. Set one stone of javelin potatoes.

Wednesday 27th April. Horsey mere. Wind fresh northerly cooler and clouds some rain later. Water has made up. Harriers about. Bearded tits. Flooding Aldreds reed.

Thursday 28th April. Jim Perrys Hickling. (30) Fine sunny day wind westerly. Shovelers about. Harriers yellow wagtails. We had to move a Robins nest out of a reed stack and put it in a hedge. We can but hope she goes to it again. Flooding Aldreds reed. 2000. [top of page is written 30]

Friday 29th April. Hickling Perrys. Wind variable cloudy at times ocaisonel showers mild. Harriers about. Several warblers here now. No crane sightings. [top of page is written 60]

Saturday 30th April. Hickling Perrys. Wind fresh easterly cloudy at times good sunny periods some light rain midafternoon warm. Some butterflies about. Several waders on the flooded marsh. Redshanks ringed plover. Several cuckoos about. Two lizards on the reed grounds. [top of page is written 105]

[Sunday 1st & Monday 2nd May] No entries.

Having a break.

Tuesday 3rd May. Horsey mere. Wind westerly fresh to strong showers cold. Several swallows and swifts martins working the mere. Lone crane flew over the mere on to the back of the hall. Young ducks near Billy Nudds mill. The crane flew out of Breydon.

Wednesday 4th May. Horsey mere. Perry. Wind fresh easterly sunny day warmer. Harriers about. Swallows swifts and martins seem happier today more food about for them. One swan on the mere looks a bit sick the lead i guess [most likely to have swallowed lead fishing weights]. Female cuckoo sitting not far from myself on some bunches of reed i tied. Feeding on the ground for a while then hopping back again. Crane came over from Horsey this afternoon and droped on Brograves marsh. A few peacocks about. Found a swallowtail chisaliss this morning in the pontoon came off a bunch of sedge. George is going to put it in his greenhouse. [top of page is written 60]

Thursday 5th May. Horsey mere Brograve. Wind fresh easterly dull start sunny later cool. Water dropping. Harriers about. Cranes have moved this year on to another marsh. Bittern flew out of blackfleet this morning and on to wet spellings. Released the dam at Brograve a wall of water came out and rubish.

Friday 6th May. Hickling Perrys. Rain in the morning fined away miday. Wind fresh easterly sunny the afternoon. Shoveler drakes chasing a duck in midair. Yellow wagtails on the marsh. Wheatear on the edge of the corn. Lizards sunning themselves on the high bank. [top of page is written 50]

Saturday 7th May. Hickling Perry marsh. Wind fresh southerly mild cloudy some sunny periods. Rained midd afternoon. One mallards nest tucked under two bunches of reed on the edge of the dyke. Covered her up again. Harriers working the marshes. No crane sightings. Several warblers here now, including a grasshopper warbler. A very good year for drinker moth caterpillars. And some others feeding near the brambles. A nice lot of violets on the edge of Perrys dykes. [top of page is written 80]

Sunday 8th May. Hickling Perrys marsh. Rain at times storm in the afternoon.

Gerald Nudd unloading bunches of sedge at Horsey Staithe.

Monday 9th May. Horsey mere. Wind fresh southerly cool rained in the afternoon. Bittern booming in Brograve marsh. Crane flew to the shud [shed] field near the hall. Harriers about.

Tuesday 10th May. Horsey mere. Brograve Mill. Wind fresh to strong south west. Showers in the afternoon heavy. Cranes flew out of Breydon and on to the potato field. Bittern booming in the Brograve marsh. The swans are still sitting hard on the west side of the mere.

Wednesday 11th May. Brograve Pump & Horsey mere. Wind light to fresh heavy showers first thing fined away sunny periods cool. Cranes flew out of Breydon and on to the potato field. One reed buntings nest five eggs in the litter bed. Little terns about. Harriers working Breydon. And some twitchers near Waxham cut. Put the dam back near the Brograve pump.

Thursday 12th May. North east side Horsey mere. Wind light variable heavy rain at times. Rained off.

Friday 13th May. Horsey mere. Wind fresh to strong south west sunny morning heavy showers and stormy midday fine away after an hour. Reed bunting sitting tight. Shorteared owl working the south side. Cormorant resting on the Island went back in the water and later came back when we were having our dinner. He seems if he could swim alright. Common terns working the mere. Water has made up a bit.

Saturday 14th May. Perry Hickling marshes. Wind fresh south west sunny periods heavy shower miday. Yellow wagtails about turtledoves odd harrier. [top of page is written 30]

Sunday 15th May. Hickling. Wind light southerly cloudy some sunny periods mild.

Sedge Warbler by Roger Nudd.

Monday 16th May. Horsey mere. Wind fresh south east fine sunny morning clouded over later showers in the afternoon and towards late evening. Sedge warblers starting to build. About fifty swans mute have turned up on the mere they seem to be getting some weed. We have not seen that amount on there for years. Harriers about. Cranes have not settled as yet. Water dropping.

Tuesday 17th May. Horsey mere. Hickling side. Wind fresh south east fine sunny day cloudy towards evening. Still about forty swans on the mere. (A black tern on the mere this morning the first we have seen for years.) Shorteared owl crossed the mere. Reports of an osprey up on the sounds. Cutting some sedge middle of Breydon not very good quality.

Wednesday 18th May. Horsey mere. Wind fresh easterly good sunny periods some cloud towards evening it has not rained now for twenty four hours. Swans seem settled here. No crane sightings. Harriers about. Bittern booming in blackfleet.

Thursday 19th May. Wind easterly fresh rained later.

Friday 20th May. Wind variable showers heavy at times. Flooded haven and flo out.

Saturday 21st May. Wind northerly fresh fine day for a change.

Sunday 22nd May. Hickling. Wind easterly fresh sunny periods. Rained late afternoon.

Monday 23rd May. Horsey mere. Wind fresh easterly sunny periods warmer at times no rain today as yet. One lone crane flew out of Breydon on to Hickling marshes. Young ducks about. Water very high unable to cut sedge.

Tuesday 24th May. Hickling Marshes. Wind fresh northerly cool fine day some sunny periods. A pair of gadwall on Perrys flooded marsh and a pair of avocets redshanks oystercatchers. One reed bunting has nested under a bunch of reed. About a little red toad have not seen one for quite some time. [top of page is written 70]

Wednesday 25th May. Wind northerly strong cool.

Thursday 26th May. Wind north west cool strong with light drizzle.

[Friday 27th May – Monday 30th May] No entries.

Tuesday 31st May. Started sedge cutting. Rain midd morning fined away later wind south east fresh a little warmer.

Wednesday 1st June. Brograve Marsh. Wind fresh south east at first veered south west later rain and a storm last thing fine afternoon. Cranes about bittern booming. About a score of swans on the mere now. Water still dropping. Recovered long line [he had gone sea fishing] this afternoon no dabs on the poll end. Could not get the anchor had to cut it away.

Thursday 2nd June. Brograve Marsh. Wind fresh at times southerly. Showers at times stormy miday. Strange bird calling in the rough sedge sounded like the one I heard late summer (Quail). Cranes active today bittern booming the end of the sedge bed.

Friday 3rd June. Brograve marsh. Wind fresh south east at first veered south west later sunny periods warmer. Water dropping. Dragonflies getting about now. Harriers about. One lone swallowtail. Twitchers about in force along Waxham cut.

Saturday 4th June. Hickling marshes. Wind fresh westerly sunny periods warm at times. Crane about harriers. Three cygnets in between the two mills.

Sunday 5th June. Hickling. Sunny morning warm. Turned cooler towards miday sea mist.

Monday 6th June. Brograve Marsh. Wind fresh easterly cool at first fine sunny later. Water very low. Marsh harriers got up right near George's feet this morning. Crane circling around the marsh. About a score of swans feeding the mere weed coming back again. No swallowtails as yet.

Tuesday 7th June. Brograve Marsh. Wind fresh south east sunny day wamer. One lone swallowtail working the end of Gibbs outlet. Crane about. Bittern on the wing. One or two more butterflies getting about now. Water very low.

Wednesday 8th June. Brograve Marsh. Wind fresh south east some cloud at first then sunny and warm later. Harrier got out again out of the sedge this morning. One reed buntings nest five young. No cranes today bittern still booming in this marsh.

Thursday 9th June. Brograve Marsh. Wind fresh south west cloudy at times cooler. Crane circling the sedge marsh this afternoon. Marsh pea coming through the rough now. Good tall sedge here now.

Friday 10th June. Brograve Marsh. Wind fresh south west variable later sunny periods. Lone crane circled over us for a few moments then went back home. Harriers about. About a score of greylags came over. The reed buntings are feeding their young quite happily.

Saturday 11th June. Wind fresh south west to stormy. Occasional light rain showers.

Sunday 12th June. Wind south west sunny periods warmer.

Monday 13th June. Brograve Marsh. Wind fresh south westerly sunny morning some cloud later water has made up four inches on this new moon. Crane left the marsh and dropped near the back of the hall [Horsey Hall]. Bittern still booming near us. Mowed in to a voles nest they all swam away to the rough sedge.

Tuesday 14th June. Wind fresh to strong westerly cool in the morning and cloudy, sunny in the afternoon and warmer. Wagtails nest in a heap of sedge on the staithes.

Wednesday 15th June. Brograve Marsh. Wind fresh northerly cloudy at first sunny later cool. Lone crane flew out of Breydon and flew over to the Waxham level came back later in to Breydon. One or two swallowtails about. Water easing. Paid John Buxton. 641 reed.

Thursday 16th June. Brograve Marsh. Wind variable sunny morning clouded over later light rain evening time. A little warmer. Crane left Breydon flew back later. A few swallowtails middle way of Breydon. George found a big one just hatched out near Waxham cut. A pair of swans feeding with two cygnets in Gibbs outlet. One or two dead fish on the mere. Water dropping a bit. But the two pumps still keep pumping the filthy ochre out. Despite it has not rained for several days now. The logic of this i dont understand.

Gerald Nudd with bunches of sedge.

Friday 17th June. Brograve Marsh. Wind fresh easterly some sunny periods warmer. Water easing. Crane came out of Breydon twice today. Bittern still having a go. Found a bearded tits nest the eggs had been sucked. One or two swallowtails about. A few dragonflies about odd horsefly. A very good year for drinker moth caterpillars.

Saturday 18th June. Hickling. Wind fresh northerly fine sunny day. Warm out of the wind.

Sunday 19th June. Brograve Marsh. Wind fresh north easterly sunny day cloudy later warm. Harriers about. No crane sightings. A few swallow tails about now. Bittern still booming now and again. Water very low pull three dam boards out [to adjust the water level].

[Monday 20th June] No entry.

Tuesday 21st June. Brograve Marsh. Wind fresh to strong north east cloudy at times some sunny periods. One fox on the edge of Gibbs outlet he saw me and vanished quickly. Harrier working the sedge bed. No crane sightings.

Wednesday 22nd June. Brograve Marsh. Wind fresh easterly cloudy morning hazy sunshine in afternoon. Storms evening and rain early morning. One reed bunting nest five eggs.

Reed Bunting by Roger Nudd.

Thursday 23rd June. Brograve Marsh. Wind fresh north easterly sunny periods. One reed warblers nest three eggs. Harriers about. Cuckoos still lurking about for nests. A few swallowtails about. Found the remains of two dragonfly nymphs which had crawled out of the water and up a sedge leaf and hatched out.

Friday 24th June. Day off.

Satrday 25th June. Wind easterly cloudy at first hazy sunshine later.

Sunday 26th June. Hazy sunshine warm day clouded over later.

Monday 27th June. Wind fresh northerly cool sunny afternoon. Water has made up a bit. A pair of marsh harriers working the marshes. Lone crane flew out of Breydon. A family of magpies at the cowsheds near Gibbs. Seen one or two swallowtails out. The drinker caterpillars are crisalising now.

Tuesday 28th June. Brograve Marsh. Wind fresh northerly sunny periods cool at first warmer in the afternoon. Harriers about. Lone crane flew out of the marsh. Rails calling in the tall sedge. Yellow wagtails on grounds we have just cleared. One or two swallowtails about. First kill of the horseflies. Norwich city variety. [yellow and green colours]
(Sprayed spuds for blight.)

Wednesday 29th June. Middle Marsh. Wind fresh northerly sunny periods heavy shower late afternoon. Lone crane left the sedge marsh and flew back later. Seven curlews flew over from Hickling marshes. One or two swallowtails about.

Thursday 30th June. Middle Marsh. Wind fresh north west sunny periods cool. Swallowtails about. A lot of black caterpillars on the nettles on Gibbs side peacocks.

Friday 1st July. Middle Marsh. Wind fresh westerly veering south west sunny periods swallowtails about now. The marsh pea is coming out now all along our track.

Saturday 2nd July. Hickling. Wind fresh south west drizzle at times mild.

Sunday 3rd July. Breydon. Fine and sunny warm fresh westerly drought. One viper [venomous snake - an adder] a bit slugish to get out of my way in our track. Several swallowtails about dragonflies getting numerous. And horseflies unfortunately. Water dropping. No crane sighting.

Monday 4th July. Breydon. Sunny day very warm fresh easterly breeze. Viper was there again this morning he moved away quickly. Herons feeding amonst the sedge stubble. Curlews about. Yellow wagtails feeding with us. Harriers about. No crane sightings water has dropped a lot.

Tuesday 5th July. Wind fresh easterly fine sunny day warm. Water low. Female marsh harrier rose up near Gibbs outlet this morning. Family of magpies and young about near Gibbs this morning . Several more butterflies getting about now. The cranes and family were heading back home this afternoon in the uncut marshes. Heading for the duckpond skulking along. I just saw one little one as they came off one rig and on to the other.

Wednesday 6th July. Breydon. Wind light easterly hazy sunshine in the morning clouded over later heavy rain in the afternoon. No crane sighting. Swallowtails about some silvery moths. One or two drinker moths about. Little red toad in the garden this evening.

Thursday 7th July. Brograve Marsh. Wind fresh easterly warm sunny day. Harriers about. Herons feeding in the holes in the sedge bed. Curlews about. Booming from the bittern in one of our tracks. A family of swans feeding on the weed in Gibbs. Some nice swallowtails about this year. One lone red Admiral flew over. Several horse flies about now. Dragon flies increasing every day now. Water still holding down.

Friday 8th July. Breydon. Wind fresh easterly fine sunny day warm. Several swallowtails about again no signs of any caterpillers as yet. The caterpillers on the nettles black ones are getting ready to chrissalize. Still one or two drinker caterpillars about. No crane sightings. Harriers about. Mowed some of the shore [dyke or river bank] of Waxham cut end weed growing fairly well pulled an eel out small on the end of my scythe. Water making just a bit. Fox near the pump on the way home. Sprayed spuds.

Saturday 9th July. Breydon. Misty start warmer later when the sun got through the fog wind fresh easterly. Water making up a bit. One swallowtail caterpiller near the hide. Several swallow tails about. Brown ringlets [butterflies] between the two pumps. [between Brograve and Eastfield] Harriers about. No crane sightings.

Sunday 10th July. Hickling. Misty day wind fresh easterly cool

Monday 11th July. Breydon. Wind fresh north east warm at times clear of mist. No signs of the cranes here they are probably safe over near Motley marsh Hickling. Harriers about yellow wagtails feeding with us. Sedge warblers feeding their young on the edge of Gibbs outlet. Swallowtails about. One or two caterpillers getting about now. Water has made up a little.

Tuesday 12th July. Breydon. Wind fresh easterly some sunny periods foggy at times.

Wednesday 13th July. Breydon. Wind fresh north east misty day. Lone crane flew across Breydon. Harriers about. Ducks bunching up. Family of oyster catchers flew over. A few more butterflies getting about now.

Thursday 14th July. Breydon. Wind fresh southerly sunny day after early morning mist very warm. Harriers working the sedge marsh. About forty mallards flew over the ducks are bunching up. No crane sightings. A few swallowtails about and a few more caterpillers. Cabbage white caterpillers coming on the greens now. One grey squirrell in our next door neighbours garden today something had been after its tail.

 Friday 15th July. Very warm. Tightened dam up and got the flat bottomed boat home to Georges. Spuds.

Saturday 16th July. Very warm.

Sunday 17th July. Very warm.

Monday 18th July. Breydon. Sunny periods warm at times wind variable. No crane sightings or harriers. Yellow wagtails about swans feeding in the outlet. Swallow tails about the caterpillers on the milk parsley are getting bigger. Spuds sprayed.

Tuesday 19th July. Breydon. Wind fresh easterly some cloud warm at times. Scratched eye badly.

Wednesday 20th July. Day off.

Thursday 21st July. Wind fresh easterly fine sunny day warm at times.

Friday 22nd July. Breydon. Wind fresh south east sunny morning cloudier in the afternoon. Warm. One bittern flew out of the marsh. Family of herons flew over. Several butterflies getting about now including the odd Tortoishell. Swallowtail caterpillers are getting bigger now. Water very low.

Saturday 23rd July. Hickling. Light showers sunny periods warm.

Sunday 24th July. Hickling. Showers first thing sunny and warm later.

Monday 25th July. Breydon. Wind fresh south east sunny and a warm day. Swallowtails about. Several other sorts. Several dragonflies now and too many horseflies. The parasitic wasps have laid the eggs on the late drinker moths now. Water has made up a little.

Tuesday 26th July. Breydon. Wind mainly easterly cloudy morning sunny afternoon warm. Harriers about working the sedge marsh reed warblers and buntings feed their young. Swallowtails about. And too many horseflies.

Wednesday 27th July. Breydon. Wind fresh at times easterly misty cooler. Kingfisher flew down Gibbs outlet first one we have seen for a long while.

Cygnets feeding on their own all day. One or two more swallowtail caterpillers now. Brought the shed home from Potterheigham George Billy myself and Roger. Brian helped to get it of the transporter. [George Newman, Billy Nicholls, Roger Nudd and Brian Applegate]

Thursday 28th July. Breydon. Wind fresh easterly cooler at first warmer later, water low. Swallowtails about marsh browns Brown ringlets. Will soon be time for the peacocks and red admiral to feed on the shores. Harrier about. No water left in this middle marsh first time for years even the deep track has dried up.

Friday 29th July. Breydon. Wind easterly very warm. Too many horse flies packed up early.

Gerald heavily laden with sedge.

Saturday 30th July. Breydon. Wind fresh easterly cloudy at times in the morning sunny very warm later. Harriers about I expect in the next few days the young will be flying. No crane sightings. Swallowtails about second hatch of caterpillers getting about. Peacocks about red admirals next week. Several butterflies between pumps.

Sunday 31st July. Hickling. Fine and sunny very warm.

37

Monday 1st August. Hickling. Rain at times wind fresh north west.

Tuesday 2nd August. Breydon. Wind fresh northerly cooler sunny period in the morning showers midday sunny later. Harriers about. One lone crane flew out of Breydon and went over to the Hall way. George saw one lone swallowtail. A few more peacocks getting about now. Odd red admiral and tortoishell. Water has made up a little.

Wednesday 3rd August. Breydon. Wind fresh northerly nice sunny day not to warm. Still a score of swans on the mere. Not too much weed this year to stop the outboard.

Thursday 4th August. Breydon. Wind fresh westerly cloudy at times good sunny periods later warm. Water has dropped a bit. The cranes have disappeared my guess that they have gone down the green twelve foot [also known as the Commissioners Drain - see map on page 10]. Harriers about. Red polls calling in the marsh. We have found one or two more larger swallowtail caterpillers. Still finding a few drinker moth caterpillers infested with the parasitic wasp larve just alive. (Sprayed potatoes)

Friday 5th August. Breydon. Wind northerly fresh nice sunny day warm. No crane sightings. Harriers about. No swallowtail Butterflies about. Found several in the middle of the marsh near some old sallows. Large ones even feeding on the young flowers of the milk parsley. Some smaller ones down on the leaves not many days old caterpillers. Several peacocks about now. Not many red admiral butterflies. Some nice water lillies near to Gibbs pump they look rather healthy. Despite the rust [ochre] Pokers looking well now on reedmace.

Saturday 6th August. Hickling. Wind northerly cool some sunny periods some drizzle first thing.

Sunday 7th August. Hickling. Wind northerly cool some sunny periods. Moved pontoon hard to beach from Lings mill [south west Hickling Broad – sometimes called Swim Coots Mill].

Lesser Redpoll by Roger Nudd.

Monday 8th August. Breydon. Wind fresh easterly cloudy at first sunny and warm later. Harriers about. No crane sightings they have moved on to the Hickling reserve where they were seen last Thursday. One swallowtail near Gibbs [outlet] this afternoon laying eggs in the parsley. Several in the middle of the marsh caterpillers feeding on the young flowers of the milk parsely. Several peacocks on the bank. Not to many red admirals.

Tuesday 9th August. Breydon. Wind fresh to strong north easterly cloudy day cooler. Water low. Harriers about ducks going about in bunches now. No crane sightings. Swallowtail caterpillers are getting larger. One or two peacocks feeding on the bank near Gibbs.

Wednesday 10th August. Breydon. Wind fresh easterly hazy sunshine at times. Water very low. Harriers about. Kingfisher flew up the outlet. George found the redpolls nest one egg left. It had been got at.

Thursday 11th August. Breydon. Wind fresh easterly cloudy morning sunny periods in the afternoon. Three marsh harriers on the wing. They have got the young one up. No crane sightings. Swallow tail caterpillers have cleared a lot of the flowers off the milk parsley. I moved two because they had run out of food. Water has made up a bit.

Friday 12th August. Breydon. Wind northerly fresh cloudy morning some sunny periods later cooler. Water has made up a bit. Harriers about. Two falcons working the marshes stayed for several minutes. The two played about in the air then diving like peregrine falcons they were young ones. The first of the Garden tiger moths today. Several peacocks about not so many red admirals. We are still finding a few more swallowtail caterpillers. The largest one are feeding up on the flowers of the parsley. Perhaps its the final fling before they Chryserliss. We have never noticed this before.

Saturday 13th August. Wind fresh northerly showers of drizle in the morning sunny periods later cool. The swans are still on the mere. Apart from when the rogue swan who has been a resident for several years. He chases them away at times. One or two dead seagulls on Hickling. Perhaps a touch of botoulism. Kingfisher working Gibbs outlet. Water has made up a bit.

Sunday 14th August. Hickling. Fine and sunny very warm wind easterly.

Monday 15th August. Breydon. Wind fresh southerly very warm water has dropped a little. Kingfisher working Gibbs all day. No crane sightings. Several peacocks about. Not to many red admirals. One lone swallowtail Waxham cut.

Tuesday 16th August. Breydon. Wind fresh to strong south west veering westerly at times sunny periods more cloudy in the afternoon. Warm. The yellow Brimstone i saw last week could have been a clouded yellow butterfly. Good showing of peacocks again to day. Harriers working the marshes. Kingfisher about. A full grown Grebe tucked in the reeds in Gibbs outlet wether he was playing dead or we hope he has not got botoulism. The weed cutter was on Horsey this dinnertime.

Wednesday 17th August. Breydon. Overnight light rain cloudy morning sunny periods later wind easterly. Cooler than of late. We found the Grebe this morning he died in the night. Lets hope it was old age. One lone crane flew over to the back of the hall. Harriers about. A few young roach in gibbs outlet. And a few young jack pike. There are still some horse flies tormenting us.

Thursday 18th August. Breydon. Wind fresh south easterly Cloudy start warm sunny afternoon. Several coots on the mere. Still a score or more swans staying on the mere. A pair of Kingfisher working gibbs outlet. Several butterflies about maghie [magpie] moths. Not a lot of sloes down the outlet. We will not fill to many bottles of gin this year. Water dropping.

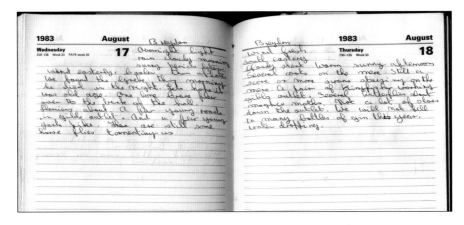

The diaries were written in a variety of different shaped year books

Friday 19th August. Breydon. Fine and sunny wind fresh easterly warm. Water low again. Harriers about. No crane sighting. Bearded tits flitting about the marsh. Clouded yellow butterfly and peacocks, painted lady odd tortoishell feeding on the Butterfly shrub in our garden this afternoon.

Saturday 20th August. Sunny and warm wind variable loading sedge for G Dunkly [Midlands thatcher].

Sunday 21st August. Breydon. Wind fresh south easterly very warm overnight rain. Just enough to lay the dust. Blackberries coming bit. Dabchicks working the outlet.

Monday 22nd August. Breydon. Wind fresh easterly sunny very warm. One blackcap in the bushes at eastfield pump. Crane calling out on the marshes. Harriers about. Several peacocks about. Not many red admirals. Still the horseflies are spitefull to us. Several dragonflies including southern hawkers.

Tuesday 23rd August. Breydon. Misty start cleared out sunny and warm miday fresh easterly winds. We have missed the swifts the last few days they have gone for another year. Cranes calling out on the marshes. Harriers about. King fisher working Gibbs. Water low. Moved gear to the sedge near the hide which should have been cut last year. Swallowtail caterpillar feeding on the flowers of the milk parsley.

Wednesday 24th August. Breydon. Wind fresh north east cloudy and cool. Sun came out latter part of the day. Grey squirrell in Borretts farm yard this morning.

Harriers about. No crane sightings. Odd bunch of teal going over water has lifted a bit now.

Thursday 25th August. Breydon. Wind fresh easterly sunny start clouded over later cooler. Swallows working low over the sedge. One pair feeding young in the hide. Linnets about. Odd wader going over. Harriers about. No signs of the yellow wagtails they seem to have gone. Wheatear near borretts farm.

Friday 26th August. Breydon. Wind fresh north east sunny periods warm. No crane sightings. Swan family feeding in Gibbs outlet. Signs of a coypu eating the reed mace roots near the crossroads in Gibbs. Swallowtail caterpillers feeding on top of the milk parsley eating the flowers and the young seeds.

Saturday 27th August. Fine and sunny.

Sunday 28th August. Cloudy and cool.

Monday 29th August. Cloudy and cool. Wind north east.

Tuesday 30th August. Breydon. Sunny and warm after cloud first thing wind easterly fresh. Swans still on the mere one score. About a hundred coot feeding on the mere the most we have seen for years. They are still cutting the weed. Dabchick feeding in the outlet. No crane sightings. Harriers about. A few peacocks about. The swallowtail caterpillar is still feeding near the hide. He is getting quite large. He has chewed all the seeds of the parsley on top and has gone down the stem to feed on the lower branches. Water very low. 300 out.

Wednesday 31st August. Breydon. Wind fresh south easterly sunny and warm. Several peacocks about on the bank , but no red admirals like we always see at this time of the year. A family of terns flew over on to the coast. Odd bunch of teal going over. No crane sightings. One dead perch Waxham cut about three quarters of a pound. Odd horse fly still around. Several blackberries. Sloe crop not very good.

Thursday 1st September. Breydon. Wind variable hazy sunshine in the morning clouded over afternoon a few spots of rain later some thunder very close. Cranes calling the far end of Breydon this morning. There seems to be more coot than the other day on the mere. Water fairly clear we could see the bottom we have not seen that for a year or two. Several peacocks about again and one or two red admirals. A lot of flies pestering us today including some horseflies. Water had made up a little.

Friday 2nd September. Breydon. Wind strong to gale south west lazy sunshine in the same showers later. Scratched my eye again. Half day.

Saturday 3rd September. Hickling. Overnight rain and in the morning sunny periods later wind strong southwest.

Sunday 4th September. Hickling. Wind fresh to strong westerly sunny periods in the morning shower afternoon.

Monday 5th September. Breydon. Wind strong westerly sunny day after some cloud first thing. Would be warm if not for this wind. Water has made up a bit.

Harriers about. No crane sightings. Peacocks about odd red admiral. No horseflies. Several yellow wagtails bunched up on the way home from eastfield.

Tuesday 6th September. Breydon. Wind fresh to strong west north west cloudy at first sunny periods later cool. Water has made up a bit. Harrier playing in Breydon no crane sightings. A family of tufted duck on the mere. Several coot still about. And a nice few swans. No bar tailed godwit sighting this year. There seem to be several signs of foxes about this year they are now feeding on black berries.

Wednesday 7th September. Wind fresh north west cloudy at times and some sunny periods. Water has made up a little. (One lone swift passed through this afternoon.) Curlews calling and water rails in the sedge. Dragon flies about. Common darters and southern hawkers. They have lost a breeding ground now the marsh is dry on this side of Gibbs.
(415 sedge on the bank) [meaning number of bunches stacked].

Thursday 8th September. Breydon. Wind fresh to strong south veering south east at times. Fine morning sunny period clouded over in the afternoon later heavy showers. Three cranes came in this dinnertimes and landed on the marshes near the outlet. Harriers about several ducks on the wing this afternoon. Water has made up again. (370 on the bank.)

Friday 9th September. Breydon. Wind fresh southerly some sunny periods some cloud. Warm at times. Odd shower towards evening. Harriers about. No crane sighting. Several duck on the wing. Water has made up a little more. None in the bed at the moment.
(240 on the bank)

Saturday 10th September. Eel Hut and the sounds [Heigham Sound]. Wind fresh to strong south west sunny periods and some showers. Several geese on the sounds. Greylag and Canada. One lone crane on Martham holms a lot of duck on the marshes and in duck broad [east side of Kendal Dyke]. Grey squirrell on the eel hut track on the way home.

Sunday 11th September. Eel hut and sounds. Showers then clear here and rained in the afternoon. Good ebb tide this morning. Several geese going over and a lot of ducks first thing feeding on the stubble.

Monday 12th September. Wind north west fresh heavy rain showers. Day off.

Tuesday 13th September. Breydon. Wind south west fresh at times some sunny periods. Water has got in to the marsh. Five roe deer near Woods duckpond [on Eastfield farm] this morning on the way down to work. Four cranes on the wing this morning. A score of yellow wagtails picking about on the sedge stubble. Kingfisher went down the outlet. A few dragonflies about. No horseflies I hope we have seen the last of them. A flock of misle thrushes on the way home picking the way through the bushes.

Wednesday 14th September. Breydon. Wind south west fresh mild hazy sunshine. Clouded over and some rain in the afternoon. Water has dropped a little. Grey Squirell in the sallow bushes. He climbed up and sat in the top of a bush and looked at us for a few seconds then scampered away. Several yellow wagtails working with us. After the insects coming out of this old sedge we are clearing. Water to high at the present to cut the better sedge. No crane sightings.

Thursday 15th September. Breydon. Showers at first sunny periods later. Wind fresh at first strong later. Showers evening time mild. Dabchicks up the outlet this morning cranes three of them landed on the Hickling marshes. Several wagtails feeding on the sedge stubble. Cleared the drains out and took the boards out water running away at the present. One lone swift flew over.

Friday 16th September. Breydon. Wind fresh south west showers at times mild. Storm middle of the afternoon. Water has made a little due to excessive pumping, wasting other peoples money. Harriers about no crane sightings. The swans have left the mere only the resident left. There must be nearly two hundred coot feeding on the mere the most we have seen for years.

Gerald Nudd on the left and George Newman gathering sedge.

Saturday 17th September. Fine and sunny at times wind fresh south west.

Sunday 18th September. Wet at first fined away miday wind south west fresh mild.

Monday 19th September. Wind fresh to strong south west sunny periods, showers light in the afternoon. Mild. Water has dropped at bit. Harrier about no crane sighting. Yellow wagtails still with us. Kingfisher working Gibbs. A few dragonflies about. Common darters.

Tuesday 20th September. Day off.

Wednesday 21st September. Breydon. Rain at times wind southerly rained heavy in the afternoon and evening. Windy blew to north west strong to gale. Several duck on the wing do to rough weather. No crane sightings. Water is making up a bit.

Thursday 22nd September. Breydon. Fine sunny day wind westerly fresh warm at times. Water making up. Harriers about. Yellow wagtails feeding on the sedge stubble. A few dragon flies about mainly common darter. Still the odd horsefly. Water making up still.

Friday 23rd September. Breydon. Wind fresh south to south east. Sunny periods warm at times water up a bit. The cranes have been over four times today one dropping on our sedge stubble in the water. Harriers out. About a score of bearded tits flying around the marsh. Kingfisher working Gibbs outlet. One red wing flew over.

Saturday 24th September. Eel Hut. Fine start clouded over the afternoon. Wind north west fresh to strong.

Sunday 25th September. Eel Hut. Wind variable fine sunny day. Several bearded tit at Kendells dyke.

Monday 26th September. Breydon. Wind fresh south west fine sunny day. Warm. Water is easing back. Lone crane flew across the sedge bed. Several duck this morning coming in from the north and teal. Harriers about. Kingfisher working Gibbs outlet. Grey squirell on the way home near Borretts farm [Eastfield Road].

Tuesday 27th September. Breydon. Wind south east fresh sunny at times. Cranes about and harriers. Curlews going through. Water dropping.

Wednesday 28th September. Breydon. Wind fresh easterly cloudy.

Thursday 29th September. Breydon. Wind fresh to strong easterly cloudy. Cranes about. Longtailed tits and bearded flocked up. Water dropping away.

Friday 30th September. Breydon. Wind fresh to strong north east cloudy and cooler. Kingfisher working Gibbs outlet feeding on the shrimps. Harriers about a dozen longtailed tits went through. Water still dropping.

Saturday 1st October. [No entry].

Sunday 2nd October. Kendell Dyke [eel set]. Fine sunny morning warm wind fresh southerly.

Bearded Tit by Roger Nudd.

44

Monday 3rd October. Breydon. Wind fresh south west showers very mild. Water low. Harriers about. Yellow wagtails still here. Two firecrest in the bushes on the way home. And a grey squirell.

Tuesday 4th October. Breydon. Wind fresh southerly warm at times sunny water has made a little. Dabchicks working the outlet. Harriers about. No hen harriers sightings yet. Cranes calling on the Horsey marshes. Dragon flies about they seem to have spread right up in to the village this year. Not many butterfly sightings.

Wednesday 5th October. Breydon. Wind fresh to strong westerly cooler. Water making up. Harriers about no crane sightings. There seem to be a few more magpies and jays about this year. And a good year for mistlethrushes. Apossum [Opossum shrimp] shrinks in our drainways. the old heron has been working on them and the kingfisher. Not any signs of coypus about.

Thursday 6th October. Wind fresh to strong westerly sunny period cool. Harriers about. Cranes calling on the marshes water rails calling near Gibbs outlet.

Friday 7th October. Wind fresh south west veered westerly later rain at times heavy later. Fined away late afternoon. Wind dropped. Water has eased a bit. Cleared all the sedge out on to the bank.

Saturday 8th October. Hickling. Wind fresh south west sunny periods and showers cooler.

Sunday 9th October. Cloudy with rain at times. Several wigeon calling in the duck broad. About thirty bearded tits flocked up near Kinders bungalow this morning. [bungalow near the eel set at Kendal dyke]

Monday 10th October. Breydon. Wind fresh south west veering westerly strong at times. Wet morning fined away to sunny miday. Water high. Still a few house martins and swallows. Several ducks about.

Tuesday 11th October. Horsey. Wind strong south west to west sunny day a lot cooler. One lone hawk near Plumers woods. Looked at a brief glance to be a hobby but couldnt be sure. Water very high. A lot of Golden plover near Horsey Corner.

Wednesday 12th October. Breydon. Wind fresh south west rain at times fined away later morning wind stronger sunny periods a little warmer. Several coots on the mere the bulk of the swans have gone a lot of duck flying about. Four cranes dropped in our sedge stubble which is flooded. Kingfisher near the staithes. Water very high.

Thursday 13th October. Breydon. Wind fresh to strong southerly sunny periods warmer rained later afternoon. Water has dropped a lot today. Several duck about. Harriers around. Kingfisher working Gibbs outlet. We havnt seen a bittern for some time now. No crane sightings. Dragonflies still about.

Friday 14th October. Breydon. Wind fresh south west sunny periods.

Saturday 15th October. Wind fresh to strong southerly rain in the afternoon.

Sunday 16th October. Wind strong to gale south west sunny at times cool. The water dropped four inches down the eel hut last night ebbed all night till dawn.

Monday 17th October. Breydon. Wind fresh to strong westerly sunny day cool. Several pigeons coming through now. No signs of the swallows and martins now. They have migrated back home. No crane sightings today. Waders coming through. Bearded tits working the reed in the sedge. Water is making up again.

Tuesday 18th October. Breydon. Overnight light rain wind south west fresh strong late some sunny periods milder. Water has not made any more. Still the odd dragonfly about. Honey suckle still flowering at the eastfield pump. Not many redwing an fieldfares as yet. Lone marsh harrier upsetting the pigeons on slaters marshes. A few mallard about. Grey squirrells being reported everywhere now. No any signs of coypus as yet.

Wednesday. 19th October. Breydon. Wind fresh at first strong later westerly cooler sunny at times. Water dropped overnight. But has made up during the day. Several duck have been feeding overnight amongst the flooded sedge stubble. Feeding on the fallen seed. There seem to be several pheasants about this year. Harriers about the odd pair of bearded tits. No crane sightings today.

Thursday 20th October. Breydon. Wind fresh westerly cool sunny periods overnight slight ground frost water still making. A few more dragon flies about again. Today common darters and southern hawkers having a last fling. A very good year for drinker moth caterpillers. Wherever we look we are finding them.

Friday 21st October. Kendell Dyke. Wind fresh northerly veering east at times cooler sunny day. Grey shrike Renolds lane Potterheigham. Two or three hundred grey lag geese on the sounds. Cormorants feeding in the tide. A few pochard. Redpolls calling in the trees there. Still the odd dragonfly about common darters. Water has not made here to much as yet.
Day off, eels.

Saturday 22nd October. Ludham. Fine sunny day.

Sunday 23rd October. Hickling. Over night frost fine sunny day.

Monday 24th October. Breydon. Wind north east sunny day some light cloud. Water making a bit. No crane sightings or harriers. Still the odd dragonfly about. A few mallard going over. Several pigeons. No grey squirrell sightings.

Tuesday 25th October. Breydon. Wind fresh south west rain at times. Sparrowhawk passed through. Dabchicks in Gibbs outlet. Meadow pippit feeding on the sedge stubble. No crane sightings. Marsh harrier upsetting the pigeons on the marshes working the stubble. No hen harrier sightings yet. Water holding its own.

Wednesday 26th October. Breydon. Wind fresh south west some rain midday. Water making.

Thursday 27th October. Breydon. Fine and sunny wind fresh south west water still making. Lone hen harrier passed through.

Friday 28th October. Wind fresh to strong northerly sunny periods showers in the afternoon. A few swans on the mere, several coot. Harriers about.

Saturday 29th October. Sunny day some cloud wind fresh north east cold.

Sunday 30th October. Wind fresh south west cloudy at times cool after overnight frost.

Monday 31st October. Breydon. Wind fresh westerly cool sunny day cloud coming in late afternoon. Harriers about no crane sightings. Goldcrests in the sallow bushes water rail swam across the outlet. Several teal about some mallard. No hooper swans here yet.

Tuesday 1st November. Breydon. Wind fresh westerly sunny period warmer in the afternoon. Water up. Dabchicks in Gibbs outlet. Harriers about no crane sightings.

Wednesday 2nd November. Breydon. Misty start cloudy later wind went south east rain late afternoon. Water making up again. Kingfisher working Waxham cut. Grey squirell back of the hall.

Thursday 3rd November. Breydon. Wind fresh misty start wind south east veered south west with sunny periods later. Water is easing back. Harriers about longtailed tit working the sallow bushes at Gibbs. Several duck on the mere. A few coot. Fieldfares coming in. Still the odd dragonfly about. Cleared the last of the sedge out and on to the banks.

Friday 4th November. Breydon. Wind south west fresh mild. Water making up.

Saturday 5th November. Castle farm Eccles. Wind southerly light misty at times. We caught four hundred herrings.

Gerald at sedge work on 3rd June 1984.

47

Sunday 6th November. Horsey Mill. Wind light and variable foggy at times clear later. Hooper swans on the mere. Cranes near bridge farm Waxham.

Monday 7th November. Breydon. Wind southeast fresh veered south west. Several crane sightings. Harriers about. Several coot on the mere. The most we have seen for years. Kingfisher working Gibbs outlet.

Tuesday 8th November. Eccles Castle farm. Wind south east fresh at times odd spot of rain. We caught about eight hundred herring today. Water very thick. Several flocks of geese going through. And several mallard. Lone shelduck.

Gerald on a pontoon at Horsey Staithe having a smoke.

Wednesday 9th November. Breydon. Misty at first hazy sunshine warm at times. Four crane sightings. Harriers about. A pair of hoopers on the mere several coot, six dabchicks in the north east bay. On the way home what we thought were harriers playing was one buzzard chased by a harrier the buzzard went and sat on the ground for a while then found a pheasant and chased him over to the Waxham level. But with little success. Water easing a little. Signs of coypus Gibbs outlet first time for a long while.

Thursday 10th November. Eccles Castle farm. Wind light misty at times but a bad swell from the east. We caught a dozen whitings. And two hundred herrings. Came in stern first rowing. Got in just in time. Several geese flying up and down the coast. Some mallard as well. We also found out the muscovy ducks eat herring. When we were not looking a big one took one and made off rather sharpish.

Friday 11th November. Horsey. Wind fresh to strong easterly cooler cloudy. Crane feeding on Plummers field near Waxham bridge farm. Four of them. Harriers about.

Saturday 12th November. Easterly fresh cooler.

Sunday 13th November. Hickling. Cool day wind fresh easterly cloudy at times some sunshine.

Monday 14th November. Breydon. Wind fresh to strong easterly cold sunny day. Cranes four on the wing to Waxham. Several ducks about. Redwings going through. Cutting the slads in the middle of Breydon. Water very low. It must have dropped eight inches over the weekend.

Tuesday 15th November. Barton Staithe. Wind fresh to strong northerly sunny periods and showers heavy towards evening. Cold but not as cold as yesterday. Helping Timmy cox repair his shed on the staithe.

Wednesday 16th November. Barton Staithe. Showers in the morning. Longer periods of rain and drizle in the afternoon. Water has made up a bit.

Thursday 17th November. Barton staithes. Wind fresh north west sunny period and showers cool. One lone bat working around the trees at barton staithes. Fish rising all along the staithe grebes fishing near.

Friday 18th November. Barton staithe. Wind light northerly drizle and rain at times milder. Repairing shed disturbed a peacock butterfly put him back under the tiles.

Saturday 19th November. Wind southerly fresh cool day.

Sunday 20th November. Wind southerly fresh sunny start showers later.

Monday 21st November. Barton turf staithe. Wind fresh north east sunny periods and showers cooler. Water rather high.

Tuesday 22nd November. Showers sunny period cool.

Wednesday 23rd November. Overnight frost sharp fine sunny day cold frost again this evening.

Thursday 24th November. Wind south east cloudy sea moderate unable to get off milder after overnight frost. Young seal on the beach having a rest. Bunches of starlings coming in. A few ducks going along.

Friday 25th November. Castle farm Eccles. Wind southerly fresh cold sunny period. Caught four hundred herring one lone dolphin cruising about near us. A few geese about and duck.

Saturday 26th November. Castle farm Eccles. Wind southerly fresh sunny periods cool. Two hundred herrings caught.

Sunday 27th November. [No entry]

Monday 28th November [No entry]

Tuesday 29th November. Frost.

Wednesday 30th November. Frost.

Thursday 1st December. Castle farm Eccles. Wind fresh southerly sunny periods cool. Got off for an hour. Two hundred herrings. Frost.

Friday 2nd December. Castle farm Eccles. Wind fresh south west sunny periods cool. Caught two hundred herrings. And a few whiting on the long line. Frost.

Saturday 3rd December. Castle farm Eccles. Wind fresh south west cool. Northern divers going up and down the coast. Lone guillemot sitting on the beach. He does not look to sharp caught fifty herrings. Frost.

Sunday 4th December. Hickling. Sunny day after overnight frost finished eels.

Monday 5th December. Mere farm Horsey. Wind fresh north west fine sunny morning rained in the afternoon. Several duck at mere farm. No crane sightings. George fell in at steam mill corner the plank broke. The reed looks a lot straiter this year on the marsh . Overnight frost.

Tuesday 6th December. Horsey corner. Started reedcutting. Wind fresh north west cold after overnight ryme frost sunny day apart from one or two showers of rain and sleet. Sea rough. One hen harrier working back of the hills. And an albino sparrow in the hall garden. Several jays and magpies about this year. Water up on the mere again.

Wednesday 7th December. Horsey corner. Wind fresh south west light rain at first after overnight frost a little milder. A pair of stonechats have been with us most of the day the first we have seen for a year or more. Marsh harrier about. There seem to be a lot of wrens about this year. Very few drinker moth caterpillers here.

Thursday 8th December. Hickling. Wet day.

Friday 9th December. Horsey corner. Wind light southerly. George moved the trailer back to Scratby. No stonechats this morning. G found out later when a crow settled in a sallow bush harassed by a sparrowhawk. Finished Horsey corner and moved inside on the marshes steam mill corner. Ready for Monday. Wind made towards evening gale force north west heavy rain at times down the eel hut. A few eels and a lot of roach. Packed up and went home in the pontoon in time for a pint.

Saturday 10th December. Hickling. Wind north west cold sunny periods and showers went shooting on Jim Perrys farm. 11 pheasants one hare. One jay. Afterwards Perry was pouring rum out as if it was going out of fashion.

Sunday 11th December. Overnight frost – sunny periods cold.

Monday 12th December. Hickling. Wet day wind south to south east drizzle then rained heavier in the afternoon.

Tuesday 13th December. Steam mill corner Marshes. Wind light southerly overnight frost. Late start. Harriers about sparrowhawk went through. No crane sightings. Meadow pipit feeding with us. A few hoopers about. Not so many drinker moth caterpillers here as on the sedge bed. Several golden plover at Horsey corner a few wigeon about.
Walked on the beach first thing sea calm one dead guillemot on the forshore a few waders on the tideline.

Wednesday 14th December. Steam mill corner Marshes. Wind fresh to strong south east cold. Some sunshine. A few hoopers about several wigeon on the mere and mallard. No crane sightings. Marsh harriers about and one hen harrier. We havnt seen a bittern for some time. Several nice bunches of golden plovers at Waxham meadows. Clearing some of the older reed up to extend this bed. Reed not to bad once we have got it in a bunch.

Gerald on a wet day - 13th October 1993.

Thursday 15th December. Wind fresh south east fine.

Friday 16th December. Steam mill corner Marshes. Harriers about several duck on the mere a few hooper. Wind fresh south east.

Saturday 17th December. Some drizle wind south east fresh mild.

Sunday 18th December. Candle dyke [sometimes written Kendell or similar spelling]. Wind fresh south east fine sunny day. Mild. Several coot about. Grey lag geese and Canada. There seem to be several cormorants about. Harrier working the sound. Reports of our cranes feeding at Dilham and Wroxham Traffords land. Aparently they came there five years ago at Dilham. The keeper Mr Ronnie Westgate said they were there for several days. Got the eel net out this morning hole in middle pod.

Monday 19th December. Steam mill corner Marshes. Wind fresh southerly mild light showers. Harriers about. A few wigeon and teal. Meadow pipit feeding with us, a pair of bearded tits. There seem to be a good few this year. And a lot of wrens.

Wren by Roger Nudd.

Tuesday 20th December. Steam mill corner Marshes. Wind fresh southerly mild rained towards miday heavy at times. Several wigeon about today. Marsh harriers about. No crane sightings.

Wednesday 21st December. Blackfleet slad. Fine sunny day mild wind fresh southerly. Harriers working the hundred acres. One Bittern flew over the first we have seen for a long while. Bearded tits about. And longtailed going through. Several duck on the mere including a few shovelers. Good growth of reed this year everywhere. A bit taller on Perrys marshes. Water dropping. Moved pontoon back to meadow dyke.

Thursday 22nd December. Fine start rained later heavy very mild wind southerly fresh.

Friday 23rd December. Eccles Beach. Wind fresh fine start rained miday fine away the afternoon. Went to sea. Fifty herrings several nice whitings and two codling on the line picked a small codling out of a low [pool].

Saturday 24th December. Eccles Beach. Wind fresh south east veering south west after overnight rain very mild sea rough on the bank.

Sunday 25th December. Wind southerly fresh very mild cloudy at times.

Monday 26th December. Wind fresh south west some cloud after overnight showers.

Tuesday 27th December. Cloudy very mild wind fresh to strong south west some sunny periods.

Wednesday 28th December. Steam mill corner Marshes. Wind fresh south west sunny day some cloud very mild. A nice flock of pigeons Horsey corner. Meadow pipit feeding with us. No stonechats. Cranes came through miday and again late afternoon. Twenty hoopers came on the mere. A few wigeon on the mere pochard teal mallard and a few shovelers.

Thursday 29th December. Steam mill corner Marshes. Wind fresh after foggy start drizle light clear afternoon cooler. To wet to cut. Sprayed the dyke out. Cranes about. Marsh harrier. One sparrowhawk. And a few hoopers.

 Friday 30th December. Steam mill corner Marshes. Fine sunny day wind north west fresh. Cooler day. No crane sightings. Marsh harrier cruising the mere. Upsetting the ducks. Geese going through to the sea. Hooper swans flying on to the mere. Good year for waterhens. A Bittern has been sleeping in the tall reed on this first marsh.

Saturday 31st December. Wind south west fresh.

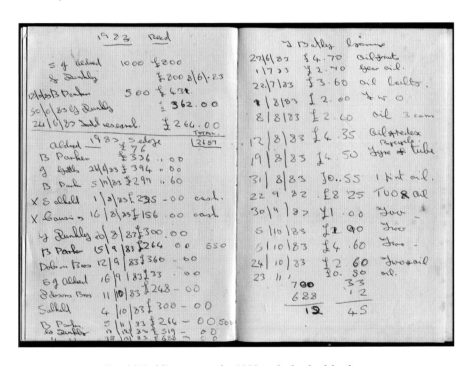

Gerald Nudd's accounts for 1983 in the back of the diary.

Left to right: Chris Nudd who had the eel set at Kendal Dyke, Gerald Nudd, Tony Batley (who at one time owned the Garage in Hickling), and Tim Cox, who had a boat on the shore in which he and Gerald went sea fishing.

Gerald Nudd, Billy Nicholls and George 'Newks' Newman.

Extracts from other years

1984

Sunday 12th February. Castle Farm Eccles. Wind light at first freshened from the east had to leave the line out caught 100 herring in a few minutes. Tried the afternoon to rough right out. Came inside shot the nets. 200 herring we did not hang long.

Wednesday 15th February...Tim Cox found the long line today.

Saturday 18th February. ..A flamingo in the flooded marsh he took off after some coots upset it. And came back later for the rest of the day he seemed quite happy feeding in the water...

Thursday 23rd February....The flamingo are still on the slads at mere farm.

Saturday 25th February. .Sleet showers and drizle. Flamingo still in the wet marsh at mere farm. He seems quite happy feeding there does not pay any attention to tractors working there…

Tuesday 28th February...Brought boat of the marshes and back to meadow dyke. Water still very low and a horrible yellow colour on the mere.

Wednesday 7th March...Crowsfoot out on Stubbs wall. And some gorse. The broom seems to be spreading a good way down the wall in the last two years. The river board will come and cut it down before long that will be the end of that.

Thursday 8th March...Three boats on the mere people pike fishing. They dont seem to be catching a lot.

Friday 16th March...One eel about. Three quarters of a pound came under the pontoon as we went down the middle of breydon. Looked like a silver eel.

Tuesday 27th March...Cranes have split up they keep coming back to Martham holms but now and again they go to Breydon leaving last years young one and the first one on the holms. Colt not moving very fast yet.

Thursday 19th April...Robins results were not to good he wants me to take his share of the eel set. And said I deserved it. Such a great pity he is a good man. [Robin Myhill had been diagnosed with cancer].

Thursday 10th May...Billy [Nicholls] and Brian [Applegate] had their reed stolen at Mautby level yesterday. [Mautby - Runham Swim way on the Bure]

Tuesday 22nd May...water to high to cut boating out. Buxton has stopped us do to the cranes.

Tuesday 29th May...Helping Paul Borret to stop a dyke caveing in near the Pleasure boat [Inn].

Monday 11th June...The Norfolk Naturalist trust have decided in their wisdom to put the price of sedge up enormously [rent for cutting sedge on their marsh]. We dont approve could price the job out…

Wednesday 13th June...No crane sightings. Several turtle doves about now and a nice lot of swifts. A few swallows and house martins. Oyster catchers at eastfield sitting on eggs near a cane for a marker in the middle of a pea field.

Thursday 14th June. Wind fresh northerly dull morning sunny later and warm. The sedge warblers are still surviving. Several turtle doves on the marsh. No crane sightings.

Monday 18th June…No crane sightings. Marsh harriers about. Swallowtail came over this marsh. Flies getting about now.

Tuesday 19th June…Bittern still booming near brograve mill. Harriers about no crane sightings. Swallowtails about. A few dragonflies and the odd horsefly.

Wednesday 20th June...Rain evening time odd clap of thunder. The swans have still got five cygnets. Greylag goose must have got a dozen goslings. No crane sightings they must have settled where they were last year. Swallowtails about.

Monday 25th June. Wind fresh northwest sunny periods warmer. The nest we left have been cleared out. Grasshopper warbler calling near gibbs outlet. One or two swallowtails about. Odd cabbage white. Water has made up sledging out.

Tuesday 26th June. Wind fresh northerly sunny periods. Warmer in the afternoon. Cranes calling near brograve mill. Bitterns still booming. Yellow wagtails about. A few more dragon flies About no horse flies. Swallowtail butterflies about. Marsh Crown Cabbage white. Water holding down.

Wednesday 27th June. ….Young cranes on kings marshes last years. Swans are surviving on the mere and a nice clutch of greylags. Grebes fishing the weed which is spreading out on the mere. Small jack pike dead in the entrance of waxham cut. The only dead fish on the mere. Reports of several dead on Hickling pike, bream and a few eels. Swallowtails about.

Thursday 28th June. …Marsh harrier working waxham level. A pair of curlews going through. Ringed plover. Not any butterflies on the wing today. Water holding down. Loading sedge this afternoon.

Friday 29th June. ….Family of swans in Gibbs outlet. Lone marsh harrier over Breydon. Found another reed buntings nest moved it into a bush newly grown over with sed. I hope they return. Swallowtails about. A few dragonflies. No horseflies thank heaven.

Saturday 30th June. ….Water making up on the new moon. Harrier working blackfleet broad. Redshanks about. Terns working the ground. Bearded tits in the tall reeds. Disturbed the barn owl out of the hut on blackfleet. He has strange company. A wrens nest and a pair of swallows. No swallowtails on this side of meadow dyke. Nearly finished the dyke for Robin myhill.

Monday 2nd July. ..Another reed bunting eggs destroyed. Found the remains of a ducks nest all the eggs had been eaten. We never used to have this trouble. I think the grey squirrels are responsible.

Tuesday 3rd July. ....Finished Robin Myhills dyke. Tony Myhill [Robin's older brother - builder] and Derek Gibbs [Amoco oil worker and Broads enthusiast] put the boathouse up [on Blackfleet Broad]. Robin was quite pleased when we saw him.

Monday 9th July...two pairs of swans clashed down Gibbs outlet. The cobs were fighting like destruction The others are not concerned at all. One family had not been hatched all that long.

Monday 16th July. Mother fell off her bike and has broken her hip.

Tuesday 17th July. ..Young cuckoo being fed by a reed bunting in the sloe bushes. Two adult cuckoos playing about there as well.

Friday 27th July. Our cat was put down today he had a growth and was going off his feet very sad. Mother will miss him very much.

Friday 3rd August. Mother came home from hospital.

Thursday 16th August...Richard Starling the volentry warden from Somerton broad came and spent a few hours with us. To see what the job was all about.

Wednesday 29th August. ..One pair of kingfishers on the edge of Waxham cut. They have been sitting on the Butterfly [yacht] early mornings. The Butterfly and her tender left for Upton dyke this afternoon. The elderly ladys holiday is over for another year. They are going back to the Isle of Wight.

Wednesday 5th September. ..The swallowtail caterpillar we found the day before was feeding on the Angelica this dinnertime. I found some milk parsley and put it near him this afternoon. He transfered on to it.

Monday 15th October. ..went fishing one small whiting on the line. Water to sheer [clear] for herring catching. A pair of gannets at sea. Skua came over . One or two birds coming in off the sea. We caught some skin divers working. The made off north at high speed in a red inflatable.

Tuesday 16th October. ..We went after some herring shot once water to sheer. No fish on the hand lines. Several geese flying up and down the coast. A few duck some teal. Great northern diver flying past. Starlings coming in fieldfares a few larks and lapwings. A pair of Chaffinches. One did not make it. Large gulls forced it down on the water.

Friday 2nd November. Robin Myhill passed away this morning at 10 o'clock. He will be missed especially down the Eel Hut.

Tuesday 6th November. Robins funeral service Hickling.

Wednesday 14th November...Packed up early and cut some reed for Cox at barton for his shed. Reed quite clean of leaf and straight.

Friday 30th November & Saturday 1st December .. Sea to rough for fishing. Took the pontoon from Meadow dyke to the eel hut.

Saturday 31st December. ..Thirty hoopers on the corn at potter Heigham. Took the eel net out covered in weed.

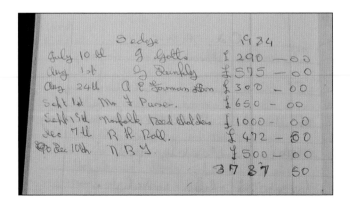

Part of Gerald's accounts in the back of the 1984 diary.

Sedge being taken to Back Dyke, Hickling Staithe.

1985

Tuesday 22nd January. ..Most of the snow has gone. The ducks and Bewicks swans on the flooded marsh are happier now. Feeding on the potatoe heaps John Buxton provided for them. Two of the hoopers have oil on them. Marsh harrier about. No crane sightings. Reed thin here but looks good in the bunch. Started back today after a fortnight off.

Monday 28th January. ...Two Bitterns near the track to mere one stood upright as me and George passed by in the car the other one flew in to the reeds John Buxton had been feeding them with spratts during the cold spell.

Friday 1st February. ...Two cock pheasants surrounded by six Magpies near Horsey corner this morning a strange sight it was.

Saturday 2nd March...We raised the Black pig [Gerald's name for the pontoon used for carting reed and sedge]... Mate Nudd died today at Sydney house [Stalham Care Home]. 90 years. [Alfred Nudd who was blind had lived in a hut near Hickling Broad]

Friday 22nd March...We went and cut the Pleasure boat [Inn] hedge down.

Tuesday 9th April. ..The board shifted on the pontoon this afternoon depositing half the load and George into the water he stayed on top and kept dry.

Wednesday 22nd May. … pike working in the weed in gibbs after fish we hope. Reports of an osprey and a golden Oriel in Potter Heigham corner on Saturday.

Thursday 20th June...John Buxton has stopped us cutting we are cutting to much sedge...

Tuesday 10th July...Cutting the Bush [Warbush area] Hickling broad.....Good cutting about here. The last time I cut this George Bishop [warden Hickling Broad at one time] was in charge twenty years ago the sedge was taller and thicker. I think this has been machined to much.

Wednesday 17th July...The cranes have been got at Horsey. Young fox got the young one. On Hickling marshes.

Monday 22nd July...Loading sedge. Jimmy Gotts [owner driver of lorry] 2000. George was filmed by the RSPB cutting sedge and sound recording.

Friday 2nd August...We left the sedge warblers a good patch they carried on feeding their young even when we were tying the sedge up along side of them...

Wednesday 6th August...A mink or grey squirrill swam the dyke and back lept out and ran along it could move very fast in the water.

Wednesday 28th August...We counted nearly one hundred and fifty peacocks [butterflies] along Gibbs outlet beside the tortoishells. One clouded yellow. And one red admiral. The swallowtail caterpillers are getting larger.

Thursday 29th August...The agro swan is at it again chasing the swans away. A good shoal of roach in Gibbs. And small pike two inches long. (42lbs pike caught at Somerton.)

Monday 2nd September...At Somerton river it was confirmed this morning the 42 pounder was caught in the river. Young cuckoo crossed the marsh this afternoon.

Tuesday 17th September...boated the last of the sedge out of horsey.The agro swan has been upsetting the other swans split them up. Both ends of the mere. Unfortunately [one of] the cobs flew from the marshes looking for them dropped in the staithe, then took off and crashed into the wires and electrocuted himself. Now we have only one pair of breeding swans. Rather sad day. Went longshoring in the evening. Eight jumbo mackerel and a few herring. The water is thicker now.

Wednesday 25th September...The coypu men caught five coypu Martham broad.

Tuesday 8th October...Stag with full antlers near Martins Marsh stubbs mill he did not seem to much concerned.

Friday 11th October...The stag and his eight hinds on the hatchet peice this morning they saw me and George jumped of the hedge onto the road and over the other hedge in to martins old marshes. They looked in good order. ..

Wednesday 4th December...Caught about one hundred longshore [herring] young seal kept helping himself...

Monday 9th December...To rough for longshoring young seal on the high water mark Eccles beach. Went after some eels later.

Wednesday 11th December. ..three large seals with us today. No sign of the young one. We caught about a box of herrings three parts small one nice whiting. We found a small gourdfish in the breakers.

Sunday 15th December. ..Sorted the eels out for smoking...We now have five crown cranes at Horsey.

Thursday 19th December...No bird report stayed home decorating.

Accounts in the back of the 1985 diary.

Whispering Reeds petrol.			
April 10th Two stroke 3 galleons		£6.	50
April 11th	1 gallon	£2	00
April 28th	2 galleons	£4.	20
May 7th	2 galleon	£4.	00
June 23rd	2 galleons	£4.	00
August 12th	3 galleons	£6.	00
August 24th	2 " "	£4.	00
August 27th	2 " "	£4.	00
Sept 3rd	2 "	£4.	00
Sept 10th	2	£4.	00
Sept 16th	2	£4.	00
Sep 20	2	£4.	00
Oct 1st	2	£4.	00
Oct 11th	2	£4.	00
		£58	**50**

Fuel expenses from Gerald Nudd's 1985 accounts.
Whispering Reeds - a boat yard at Hickling.

Gerald Nudd scything sedge in the heat of the summer.

1986

Friday 21st February. Wind light easterly snow showers sharp overnight frost. Shot seven pigeons on James Perrys he gave me a glass of brandy with my coffee enough to kill a horse. I only went to see him to borrow some cartridges...

Saturday 17th May... Runham Swim [near Mautby on the Bure]. Cleaning the reed up and loading Parker in the afternoon. Mink have bred under the heaps of reed two lots...one mink came out of a heap of reed.

Friday 13th June...John Buxton is cutting us back on the sedge wishing to leave some for four years and requested us to clear some rough stuff along the Hickling wall hard work done for nothing.

Tuesday 17th June...sunny very warm the warmest day for year packed up miday...

Wednesday 18th June...Billy Nicholls has sunstroke.

Friday 20th June...Moved to the hides sedge short and thin. Such a pity we have got to leave good sedge all the clearing we have done has gone to pot. John Buxton makes a mockery of conservation. Crane on borrets hay field the young quite big now.

Saturday 21st June...went to pleasant hill [Pleasure Hill, east Hickling Broad] with the warden Stewart Linsell. Sedge not to bad on pleasure hill one or two dead bream about. a disastrous week a fox cleared the terns and redshanks 16 terns common nests 3 redshanks. Crows got the advocets eggs....

Wednesday 25th June...John Buxton has lost the crane but we know where they are? Weed blocking Waxham cut floated down from the weed cutting operations.

Friday 27th June... the bittern flew out of Brograve marsh they must have young he goes out quite regularly. Cranes in borrets corn on the way home. And moved off quickly. The reason we found out in seconds. The young one was on the dyke and dashed in missing us by a yard. The hen came back to it. We did not stop to look, we let them get on with it as we usually do. I dought wether John Buxton has ever been as near as we were.

Friday 4th July...Horsey. Lone crane came over. The bittern is working these two marshes regularly. We hope they are feeding young. Curlews coming through. Flight of mallard on the wing. A heron and a marsh harrier having a dog fight over breydon it last for quite sometime. The trials on prymnesium have been fairly successful using aquias ammonia on hickling. The trust as usual are burying their head in the sand all they think of is birds.

Friday 18th July. Wind fresh and cool fine sunny day light clouds. Water has made a bit. Marsh harrier quartering breydon. No crane sightings. Bearded tits feeding second hatch. And reed buntings Blue tits feeding in the sallow bushes. Young pheasant flew out of the corn. Good crop of weed in gibbs outlet. The water lilies are not doing to bad this year.

Saturday 19th July. Wind fresh south west sunny periods more cloud today Wroxham river Grebe fish amongst all the traffic Greylag geese dodging as well. Yellow water lillies out near a old boat house It is marvellous how they survive all the wash pollution.

Gerald relaxing in a friend's house.

At this point the note book diary entries stop. There is a gap until they begin again later in the year written on sheets of loose leaf paper. The entries with some gaps, now become simpler and do not always begin in the normal way with a weather report. Here, as written, are the remaining entries beginning at the end of October and ending in January 1987.

Monday 27th October. Wind fresh south west cloudy some rain heavy in the afternoon. Lone dabchick working gibbs outlet. A dozen hooper swans came off the Waxham level the first this year. A lot of duck over the mere several geese. No cranes about. Still no eels at the Waxham pump. Water very high in breydon. Day off.

Tuesday 28th October. Rain at first clearer later rained again evening wind south west fresh. Day off. Tortaishell in the garden.

Wednesday 29th October. Hickling Broad. Wind fresh to strong south west sunny. Boating sedge up to hickling staithe. Several duck on the broad and geese Canada and greylag. A few commorants. Snipe on the sedge ground. Grebes about. A few wrens about in the rough sedge. No bearded tits today. Water has dropped.

Thursday 30th October. Wind strong to gale south west sunny morning mild cloudy afternoon drizzle showers. Reports of a perergrine falcon Somerton has been here for several days now. Boated a small load of sedge up a bit of a job in all this wind. Caught a eleven pound pike in the gear eel set. Bat working around the eel hut at dusk.

Friday 31st October. Wind fresh south west sunny at times cloudy late afternoon. Water has dropped. Strange goose down the eel set sometimes he nearly cuckoos when he calls lone canada goose. Three cranes on the Waxham marshes this morning. Marsh harrier about. Sixteen long tailed tits working the sloe bushes gibbs outlet. Grey squirrel at gutemere this morning [Guttermere is an area Hickling side of Catfield dyke]. One small eel in the gear Brograve pump Waxham a few sticklebacks.

Saturday 1st November. Wind northerly gale force heavy rain at times cold water very high.

Sunday 2nd November. Wind northerly cool sunny at times.

Monday 3rd November. Wind light south west fine and sunny. There seem to [be] more coots on hickling broad this year.

Tuesday 4th November. Kendell dyke. Wind light south west frosty morning. Marsh harrier sitting on an old tree stump he watched me steam past. Another working pleasure hill where we cut the sedge.

Wednesday 5th November. Wind fresh south west cloudy start sunny later. Went longshoring one herring on sprat for three shoots. Barnacle goose came past. Three fieldfares came in, and a few starlings they had a good punch across. Lone guillemot feeding near the nets.

Thursday 6th November. Kendell dyke. Wind light south west fine sunny day frost evening time water still high. Four dabchicks working near the set [eel set]. Several golden plover on Martham holms. A lot of starling weaving about over the holms then headed for the hundred acre, where they are resting on the trust reed in their thousands. They cannot shift them by any means. Cetties [Cetti's] Warbler calling near the set.

Saturday 15th November. Wind light south west went herring catching half a box. Not longshores big herrings. A lot of duck resting on the sea   grebes about.

Monday 17th November. Wind fresh south west. Mild wet later.

Tuesday 18th November. Fine day rained later nineteen herrings for six hours work. Several brent geese at sea grebes feeding near the shore. Two seals here the first we have seen for a long while water thick. Still a few fieldfares coming in.

Wednesday 19th November. Fine at first cloudy later wind strong to gale south west. No eels.

Thursday 20th November. Sunny at times wind fresh south west. Rained evening time cooler.

Friday 21st November. Kendell dyke. Cloudy at times wind light at first then came north west showers fresh hanging west at times. Lone marsh harrier over Martham holms. Cetties warbler has made his home near the eel set. Dabchicks about. Cormorant popped up right near the pontoon this morning. He was surprised. More coot on hickling broad than people think.

Saturday 22nd November. Kendell dyke. Wind fresh to strong southerly cooler sunny day. Several golden plover on these marshes. Twenty bewicks passed through Cormorants working the set here must be after the roach moving up. The cetties warbler has made his home here now.

Sunday 23rd November. Wind strong south west some rain early.

Monday 24th November. Wind fresh south west cloudy mild. Marsh harrier about and hen harrier. Lone bittern rose up out of Gibbs outlet. One small silver at the brograve pump.

Tuesday 25th November. Wind still strong south west.

Wednesday 26th November. Fine and sunny mild.

Thursday 27th November. Wind light south west sunny mild. 79 hooper swans came over Potterheigham marshes.

Friday 28th November. Wind light south west fine sunny day caught thirty herring Two seals working the gear. One lone fieldfare coming in he made it. Grebes feeding near the shore.

Saturday 29th November. Cold thick fog all day. Sun came through odd times. To thick to go to sea.

Sunday 30th November. Kendell dyke. Fog cleared overnight. Wind cold south west Cetties warbler calling near the eel set. About two hundred canada geese came over. Marsh harrier working swim coots [marshy land and part of Hickling Broad south]. Water still holding down. Took the eel net out.

Monday 1st December. Went to sea caught a nice lot of shrimps a box nearly in two hauls, Several small whiting small dabs, soles, bullheads two sprats in the shrimp trawl. Wind fresh south west mild some cloud about.

Tuesday 2nd December. Wind fresh south west fine sunny day mild no work.

Wednesday 3rd December. Wind fresh to strong west sunny mild Loading sedge hickling staithe.

Thursday 4th December. Wind fresh to strong south west cloudy mild. Cutting Teddy Bishops hedge down nearest the road. Now James Perrys. Good pieces of thorn. [Teddy Bishop, local builder]

Friday 5th December. Wind fresh south west mild Lone sparrow hawk came through. A few pigeons about.

Saturday 6th December. Overnight frost wind light south west. Fine sunny day. The fieldfares are now starting to feed on the white thorn hibs.

Sunday 7th December. Wind fresh south west sunny at times mild.

Monday 8th December. Very wind[y]. south west gale.

Tuesday 9th December. Very windy south west gale.

Wednesday 10th December. Fine and sunny water has made up a bit. Wind fresh southerly Found a dead tawny owl on the big rond. He had not been dead long remains of two starlings he had eaten the night before.

Thursday 11th December. Cloudy and cool rained miday.

Friday 12th December. Fine and sunny after overnight frost wind fresh southerly. The fieldfares and black birds are working solid on the large hedge of teddy bishops pity it is coming down.

Saturday 13th December. Rain at first fine later and sunny wind fresh south west.

Sunday 14th December. Kendell dyke. Wind light southerly. Fine sunny day after overnight frost. Water making up again several greylags on the marshes here. Lone marsh harrier cetties Warbler calling. Counted a dozen cormorants from hickling to the sounds. Must be enough fish for them.

Monday 15th December. Rained all day wind strong southerly.

Tuesday 16th December. Wind fresh to strong southerly cool overnight frost. Sunny day. Chaffinches about. Several pigeons on Perrys corn. A lot of fieldfares on the white thorn now.

Bittern and young.

Common Crane and family photographed by John Buxton.

1987

Thursday 1st January. Wind strong westerly rained all day.

Friday 2nd January. Wind fresh south west cloudy rained morning for the rest of the day. Finished the reed fence the bolt Kendell dyke.

Saturday 3rd January. Fine and sunny cool wind fresh south west.

Sunday 4th January. Wind south west fresh rained most of the day.

Monday 5th January. Wind fresh north west strong sunny cold water high. Some reed at ling mill hickling. water high some left in from last year.

Tuesday 6th January. Cloudy cool some light showers. Wind northerly cold.

Wednesday 7th January. Started reed cutting. Wind fresh northerly some sunny periods. Heavy hail shower mid morning. Took the gear from meadow dyke and on to cubbits marsh Mere farm marshes. Cranes about a few hoopers about several ducks in the flooded marsh. Lone kestrel sat in a bush looking at me a few yards away as if I did not belong there. Picked a nice mallard drake out of meadow dyke found another one on the way home the rats had been at him slightly. They were shot last night. The water is high on this marsh. (30)

Thursday 8th January. Rhyme frost at first Cleared mid morning. Wind light north west. About nine bearded tits working here on cubitts marsh and a pair of water rails. Marsh harriers about. (40)

Friday 9th January. Frosty all day the rhyme never came off the reed. (69)

Saturday 10th January. Wind strong to gale northerly overnight frost I think there is some bad weather coming.

Sunday 11th January. Wind strong north east some overnight snow. Very cold.

Monday 12th January. Wind fresh north east a little more snow showers on and off all day severe frost.

Tuesday 13th January. Wind fresh north east. More overnight snow it has now started to drift. We have about six inches now. Looks very bad for the next few days.

Wednesday 14th January. Very cold still drifting wind strong north east.

Thursday 15th January. Wind easing. Light now roads still blocked.

Friday 16th January. Overnight frost wind light variable.

Saturday 17th January. Some sunshine a slight thaw.

Sunday 18th January. Cloudy. thawing.

Monday 19th January. Cloudy some drizzle. thawing a bit more.

Tuesday 20th January. Cloudy some drizle. some fogg.

Wednesday 21st January. Cloudy at times wind light northerly.

Thursday 22nd January. Over night fog snow going wind northerly. the [sun] shone odd times Started reed cutting inside marsh near steam mill corner. Several ducks resting on the mere and Bewicks. Marsh harriers about. Lone bittern rose out of the marsh near meadow dyke. Pulled chrisses nudds boat up the outlet on the ice and crossed near the soke [dyke] which goes in to blackfleet broad. [In side margin is written (25)].

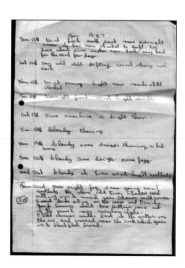

The last page of Gerald Nudd's diary - finishing on Thursday 22nd January 1987.

Mr G.R Nudd

Mr Gerald Robert Nudd, of The Green, Hickling, has died at his home in the village where he was born 58 years ago.

Part of his life was spent at sea, later he was a marshman and reed cutter working for 30 years on the Hickling Estate.

He was a son of the late Charles and Evelyn Nudd and is survived by his brothers Michael, Roger and Austin, one niece, two nephews, a great-nephew and a great-niece.

The funeral service and burial at St Mary's Church, Hickling, were conducted by the Rev W J Cameron. Mrs N Brindid was the organist.

Family mourners were Mr and Mrs Michael Nudd, Mr and Mrs Roger Nudd (also representing Emma), Mr Austin Nudd, Mrs Jacqueline Shaw (Mr Andrew Shaw), Mr and Mrs Christopher Nudd (Elisha) and Mr Darren Nudd.

Others attending included Mr D Adams and Mrs J Adams, Mr J Meale, Mr B Beales, Mr K Beales, Miss R Perry, Mr R Perry, Mr D Morris, Mr C Peake and Mrs P Peake, Mr T Stringer and Mrs L Stringer, Mr D Haylett, Mr R Warrell, Mr M Folds, Mr T Mayes, Mr and Mrs J Perry, Mr M Thompson, Mr J Hales, Mr B Roberts, Mr N Belson, Mr R Attew, Mr and Mrs C Clarke.

Mrs J Amis (Mr B Amis), Mr and Mrs H Nudd, Mr G Taylor, Mr P Nudd, Mr and Mrs J Aldred, Mr C Nudd, Mr D Platten (Mrs M Platten), Mr L Pye, Mr H Beales, Mr and Mrs G Mitchell, Mrs L Applegate (Mr M Blount and Mrs J Blount), Mrs S Prime (Mr M Prime), Mr and Mrs D How, Mr G Newman, Miss D Utting, Mr M Lawes, Mr C Adams, Mr D Beales, Mr and Mrs D Mayhew, Mr and Mrs G Mayhew, Mr B Lawton and Mrs J Lawton, Mr S Golby and Mrs J Golby, Mr S Beales, Mr T Patterson, B and S Village Shop, Mr J Tallowin and Mrs N Tallowin, Mr G Amis, Mr I Mayhew, Mr J Blaxell (Mrs E Blaxell), Mrs P Robinson, Mr D Jenkin, Mr and Mrs P Crook.

Mr G Howarth, Mr D Elliott, Mr B Applegate, Mr and Mrs D Tate, Mr and Mrs G Turner (Mr and Mrs David Nudd), Mr J Blackburn (Norfolk Wildlife Trust), Mrs B Myhill, Mrs U Stapleton, Mrs J Gething, Mr and Mrs R M Starling, Mr B Ellis, Mr R J Scott, Mr N Moody, Mr D Cator, Mr J Parsons, Mr R Brooks, Mr B Beales, Mr F Tillett, Mrs J Sheppard, Mr D Applegate, Mr C Shingles, Mr A Beales, Mr and Mrs R Gibbs, Mr S Allison, Miss E Beales, Mrs J Allen, Mrs J Waters, Mr and Mrs C Stimpson, Mr and Mrs T Brookes, Mr and Mrs B Brookes, Mr and Mrs W Nicholls, Mr D Nudds and Mrs J Nudd.

Mr B Amiss, Mr T Newman, Mr J Crook, Mr P Burdett, Mr M Toll, Miss C Stapleton, Mr P Burnett and Mrs M Burnett, Mr L Beales (Mrs D Beales and Mr L P Beales), Mrs V Purdy, Mr A Haylett, Mr R Benjamin, Mr and Mrs K Smith, Mr and Mrs J Artis, Mrs I Clark (Mr G Clark), Mr I G Baxter-Pownall (Mrs A Baxter-Pownall), Mr A Woodman, Miss D Key, Mr S Wren, Mr S Morgan and Mrs C Morgan, Mr C Seward, Mr V Wilding, Mr A Barker.

Newspaper cutting from the North Norfolk News of 18th February 1999.

Gerald Nudd 1940-1999

Gerald Nudd died in his home at No. 7 The Green, Hickling, on 13th January 1999. He was 58 years old. So many people attended his funeral service a month later in Hickling Church that they could not all get in. His grave was adorned with bundles of reeds and many flowers. The funeral was reported in the *North Norfolk News* of the 18th February. Virtually all of Hickling was there, along with family members, friends and colleagues from other villages and towns across Norfolk.

Gerald Nudd's grave in Hickling churchyard, February 1999.
with a fathom of reed resting on a boat shaped design.

People who knew Gerald remember him as a kind and caring person. Richard Starling, fellow reed and sedge cutter at Martham, said "George, Billy and Gerald ended up at Martham as they were prevented from cutting sedge at Horsey in case they disturbed the nesting cranes. I have some very happy memories of all three and they really did work very hard, caring for the environment and people."

Paul Borrett, who took over Eastfield Farm from his father and ran it until 2005, writes "In the past there were many Hickling men who earned a living independently doing various seasonal jobs - herring fishing; singling sugar beet; lifting, knocking and topping sugar beet; corn harvesting; reed cutting etc. They were hard working, very tough men and Gerald was one of a kind.

"They worked as did Gerald as long as the weather was kind, and when it was bad you could usually find a few of them in the pub, and Gerald was no different.

"Gerald did have a wonderful knowledge of wildlife, and knew the area in and around Hickling and Horsey Broads like the back of his hand. When he came through my farmyard as he did many times when working on Brayden Marshes he often stopped and had a chat about the wildlife around at the time. Gerald Nudd was a most interesting man - as we would say in Hickling - a good old boy."

James Perry, who took over his mother's Poplar Farm, and also had some fields and marshes near Stubb Mill, said "One of his favourite things was when he found the Marsh Pea in a place called 'Dead Man's Hole'. Nobody had ever seen it before. He never picked it, just left it for next year.

He was just a man who loved his work and nature. One of his favourite sayings was 'You'll miss me when I am gone'. He was right. A real character. He could turn his hand to anything."

The last word must come from Gerald's brother Roger Nudd, who kept Gerald's diaries and notes, and without whose help this book would never have been possible.

"Gerald was a wonderful man, everybody liked him. Nobody spoke bad of him, never have done. He looked after his parents to the end. To do all that, and work, and socialise - he worked very hard. Him and George, a lovely man, in the summer time that's light just after five, they'd be off cutting sedge, they would be finished by lunchtime. Gerald used to dress up from time to time. My mother used to say 'what is he up to now, dressed up with a tie on, where's he going'. My eldest brother Michael said he had been a really good man. He was a one off."

Gerald Nudd's grave in Hickling Churchyard.
His life was the marsh, he learnt its ways over a lifetime.

Gerald Nudd with William Nudd on the left photographed in 1991 at Hickling Staithe. William, known as Billy Nudd [1908-1993] looked after Stubb Mill, also known as Nudd's Mill, pumping water off the Hickling marshes into Meadow Dyke until the sails fell off the mill in 1930. Subsequently the mill was operated by a steam engine until it was replaced by a diesel operated pump in 1940. Now the pump is operated by electricity but still does the same job as the mill had done since it was built in 1805.

Stubb Mill, also known as Nudd's Mill, photographed in August 2019.
This pumped water off the Hickling marshes to Meadow Dyke.

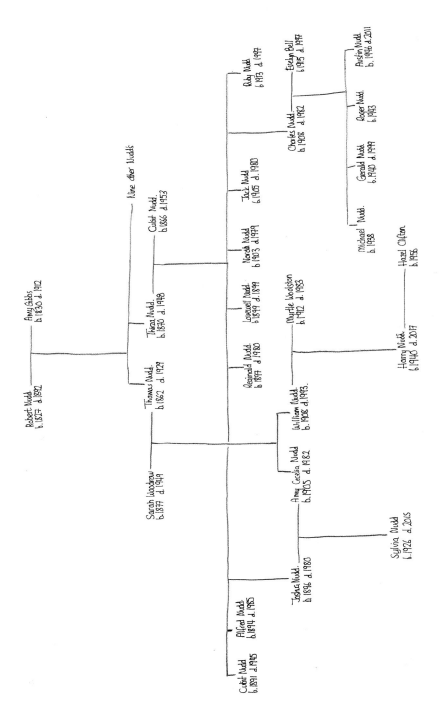

Robert Nudd
b.1827 d.1892

Amy Gibbs
b.1830 d.1912

Nine other Nudds

Sarah Woodrow
b.1877 d.1949

Thomas Nudd
b.1862 d.1929

Tirza Nudd
b.1870 d.1948

Cubit Nudd
b.1866 d.1953

Cubit Nudd
b.1891 d.1945

Alfred Nudd
b.1894 d.1985

Joshua Nudd
b.1896 d.1980

Amy Cecelia Nudd
b.1905 d.1982

William Nudd
b.1908 d.1993

Reginald Nudd
b.1897 d.1980

Lovewell Nudd
b.1899 d.1899

Norah Nudd
b.1903 d.1979

Jack Nudd
b.1905 d.1980

Ruby Nudd
b.1913 d.1999

Sylvia Nudd
b.1926 d.2015

Myrtle Woolston
b.1912 d.1983

Harry Nudd
b.1940 d.2017

Hazel Clifton
b.1956

Michael Nudd
b.1938

Gerald Nudd
b.1940 d.1999

Roger Nudd
b.1943

Charles Nudd
b.1908 d.1982

Evelyn Bell
b.1915 d.1997

Austin Nudd
b.1946 d.2011

Where Gerald Nudd fits in with his immediate family members and past history.

75

This phototaken by Mike Page shows the Thurne and Martham Ferry, Kendal Dyke, Duck Broad, Heigham Sound, Whiteslea, Hickling Broad, Meadow Dyke, Blackfleet Broad, Horsey Mere, and in the bottom right-hand corner Martham (Somerton) Broad.